SPECIAL INTEREST GROUPS IN AMERICAN POLITICS

SPECIAL INTEREST GROUPS IN AMERICAN POLITICS

STEPHEN MILLER

With a Foreword by
Irving Kristol

Transaction Books
New Brunswick (U.S.A.) and London (U.K.)

Copyright © 1983 by Transaction, Inc.
New Brunswick, New Jersey 08903

Library of Congress Catalog Number:83–4691

ISBN: 0–87855–485–8 (cloth)

Printed in the United States of America

Library of Congress Cataloging in Publication Data

Miller, Stephen, 1941–
  Special interest groups in American politics.

  Includes index.
  1. Interest groups—United States—History.
I. Title.
JK1118.M55   1983   322.4'3'0973   83–4691
ISBN 0–87855–485–8

TO MY MOTHER AND FATHER

Contents

Acknowledgments

I am indebted to many people for assistance in the preparation of this book. Midge Decter, Leslie Lenkowsky, Irving Kristol, and Irving Louis Horowitz made many useful suggestions after having read the first or second draft of the book. I also benefited from numerous conversations with Robert Licht, Walter Berns, and Michael Malbin. Anne Miller and Gabriele Hills helped with the typing. Parts of this book, in somewhat different form, have appeared in *The American Spectator* ("Mugwumps Today," April 1980) and in *The Public Interest* ("Adam Smith and the Commercial Republic," Fall 1980).

Foreword

Irving Kristol

The popularity of the term "public interest" and the proliferation of groups with an official dedication to the public interest are among the most striking phenomena of the past two decades. An associated phenomenon is the disrepute into which such terms as "private interests" or "special interests" have fallen.

It is impossible to imagine a society—the world does not know of a society—without some prevailing conception of the public interest, otherwise known as the common good, *res publica,* the common weal, the general welfare, etc. A society is based on a shared way of life, in turn based on shared values, which in turn tends to legitimate one form of political authority rather than another. And this authority must behave in a manner consistent with the society's way of life and values. Out of this interaction there emerges a notion, however nebulous, of a public interest.

I have noted that the "public interest" is only one term among many for this phenomenon. These different terms have different shades of meaning that are significant, for they point to shifting emphases in self-definition associated with various types of social, economic, and political regimes. The use of "general welfare," for instance, suggesting as it does the aggregated welfare of individuals, is instinctively felt to be more appropriate to the United States today than "common good," which hints at possible divergence of the two welfares. Indeed, when a democratic politician speaks of promoting the general welfare, we expect him to do things for our benefit, while if he speaks in the name of the common good we suspect he is going to be demanding sacrifices of us.

What the "public interest" *means* for any particular society, at any moment in its history—is the task of political philosophy to study and explore. Unfortunately, this is a task that political philosophy in our day is peculiarly impotent to perform. This is because the two founders of modern theory of the "public interest"—Machiavelli and Rousseau—point us, each in his own way, in the direction of blind alleys.

Machiavelli is the first political theorist—in the West at any rate—who
simply dismisses the possibility of anything like a viable idea of the public
interest, common good, common weal, or anything of the sort. Or perhaps
one should say, more exactly, that it was his teachings as handed down
through generations of political theorists that became so dismissive, since
there is reason to believe that Machiavelli himself felt the keenest nostalgia
for the ancient Roman ideal of a collectivity oriented around a firm ideal
of the *res publica,* to which each and every citizen subordinated himself. But
Machiavelli was persuaded that the advent of Christianity, with its emphasis of the individual's relation to the Deity, as distinct from a predominantly
civic religion, had shattered that ideal beyond repair, and that in the world
of modernity, both the world he lived in and foresaw, politics was nothing
but the arena in which private interests, individual and class, struggled for
hegemony.

Out of this teaching there emerged that tradition of political theory
associated with such names as Hobbes, Locke, Hume, and Bentham. It is
the tradition that dominates twentieth-century "political science," which
analyzes politics as nothing more than the complex interaction of self-
interested individuals—whether rulers, legislators, or citizens—as well as of
self-interested groups or classes. It is also the tradition that gives rise to the
modern science of economics, which concedes reality only to the sovereign
individual's preferences, appetites, and desires. While it is possible to aggre-
gate these preferences, appetites, and desires—to move from microeconom-
ics to macroeconomics—this aggregation is purely statistical and has no
normative connotations. Some of our finest economists have tried very hard
to derive a "social welfare function"—an economist's version of the common good—from the process of aggregation, but it seems to have been
demonstrated that this is logically impossible.

In his political writings Rousseau tried to annul the distinction between
individual self-interest and public-spiritedness by establishing a civic religion. By strictly shaping the minds and wills of each individual, this new
orthodoxy would create and sustain a society in which all individuals
voluntarily and unanimously chose the public interest as being their true
self-interest. This ideal is obviously utopian; even in their halcyon days, the
Greek polis and Roman republic did not achieve any such reconciliation.
But it is an ideal, nevertheless, that is at the heart of all modern collectivist
and totalitarian movements, whether of the Right or Left. Inevitably, such
movements end up destroying individual liberty and legitimating a political
system in which an elite, as presumptive representatives of "the people,"
rules more or less despotically.

In between these two extreme intellectual tendencies there has emerged
in the West an interesting and fruitful compromise, one that has worked

extraordinarily well in practice but which has been less well articulated as a distinctive way of thinking about the proper relation of self-interest and public interest, of balancing a concern for individual liberty with a recognition of the fact that arrangements must be made—in the political system, the educational system, the religious institutions, etc.—so that the self-interest that is an expression of individual liberty will be refined and "enlightened." This intellectual tradition is associated with such names as Montesquieu, the authors of *The Federalist,* and Tocqueville. It is a "liberal" tradition—though, as seen through the eyes of modern Left liberalism, it appears "neoconservative"—that seeks to authenticate a middle way, along which a democratic capitalist way of life can move with good conscience and good effect, a way of life in which the inevitable tension between regard for self and regard for the common weal is fruitfully mediated.

In recent decades, this tradition has not received the study and attention it merits, so that the self-understanding of democratic capitalism has become impoverished. Stephen Miller's book, therefore, is an important and welcome contribution to American political thought. Those who read it will have a better understanding of why American democracy has been as successful as it has been, and why the absence of such an understanding today is weakening the very foundations of American democracy.

Introduction

Attacking special interests is as American as apple pie. In his farewell address to the nation, Jimmy Carter said that "special interest organizations" are "a disturbing factor in American political life." The national interest "is not always the sum of all our single or special interests. We are all Americans together—and we must not forget that the common good is our common interest. . . ." In his inaugural address, Ronald Reagan made essentially the same point: "We hear much of special interest groups. Our concern must be for a special interest group that has been too long neglected," by which he meant all Americans. Both Carter and Reagan were echoing Senator Edward Kennedy, who said in 1978 that "the Senate and the House are awash in a sea of special-interest contributions and lobbying." Republicans and Democrats, conservatives and liberals, politicians of all persuasions have attacked special interests. And most Americans agree with them that special interests are thwarting the will of the people. According to a 1980 poll, an overwhelming majority (84 percent to 12 percent) is convinced that "special interests get more from the government than the people do."[1]

During recent years, these attacks probably have increased in frequency. Early in his 1984 presidential campaign, Walter Mondale called for the Democratic party to "declare a war on special interests," and he also said that he would not accept any campaign contributions from them. (Another presidential candidate, Senator Gary Hart, took the same stand.) The denunciation of special interests, however, has been a commonplace of American political rhetoric since the beginning of the Republic. In 1777 Samuel Adams was reflecting the sentiments of many when he worried that the people of Boston might "soon forget their own generous feelings for the Publick and for each other as to set private Interests in Competition with that of the great Community."[2] Americans have continuously worried that the power of special interests—or what Adams called private Interests— was making it difficult to pursue what Jimmy Carter called "our common interest."

In attacking special interests, politicians are catering to the pervasive

1

suspicion of many Americans that Congress is composed of venal or corrupt men. Opinion polls regularly show that Americans rate the honesty and ethical standards of congressmen quite low compared with members of other professions. When Mark Twain said that "there is no distinctively native American criminal class except Congress," he was referring to the Congress of the Gilded Age—supposedly a time when special interests bought the votes of many congressmen. But Americans have always been inclined to assume that power is a corrupting force. Colonial Americans, Edmund Burke said, are a suspicious lot who "snuff the approach of tyranny in every tainted breeze."[3] After independence, many Americans retained their mistrust of government and worried about corruption as well as tyranny. For a goodly number the two went hand in hand; national legislators, they often said, must be watched vigilantly lest they become corrupt, conspire against the public interest, and subvert the liberties of the people. The suspicion of national legislators has been a potent force in American politics, manifesting itself in recurrent drives by reformers to reduce the influence of special interests, and manifesting itself also in candidates for congressional office who imply that they—unlike the incumbents—are not corrupt because they have not been in office. According to a recent poll, only 18 percent of the public has confidence in Congress, and most Americans are convinced that "the people in Washington are out of touch with the rest of the country."[4] What most Americans probably think about congressmen was summed up by an Iowan Jonathan Raban met on his trip down the Mississippi: "Them politicians, they're a bunch of outlaws. You know the only thing those guys in Washington ever agree about is giving themselves pay hikes?"[5]

So commonplace has been the practice of attacking special interests in particular and political corruption in general that Sacvan Berkovitch in *The American Jeremiad* (1979) calls such political sermonizing a patriotic rite, a national custom that has been a unifying force in American life. Why not, then, simply dismiss such attacks as the cant of politics—the stock in trade of politicians who hope to avoid discussions of particular issues by declaiming about the evils of special interests?

Complaints about the power of special interests, however, cannot be set aside as so much political blather, for during the past ten years even politicians and political observers who defend the legitimacy of special interests have become worried about the "extraordinary flowering of special-interest pressures in Congress." Virtually all observers agree that there has been a tremendous political mobilization of interest groups in our society in the last decade. In 1974, 1,146 groups contributed $12.5 million to congressional campaigns; in 1980, 2,551 groups gave $55.3 million; and in 1982, 3,479 groups gave an estimated $80 million.[6]

Lobbyists for special interests can certainly make a politician's life difficult. "They come at you in relays," Senator Daniel Patrick Moynihan of New York relates: "It's like the human wave approach to legislation. They never stop." Yet some observers, including many congressmen, think lobbyists are very useful. They help to clarify and define the debate about a particular bill. They provide information to congressmen who are too harried to get it for themselves. As an observer put it in the *New York Times:* "Members of Congress admit that they depend upon lobbyists to brief them on issues. . . . They listen to lobbyists representing more than one side of an issue and proceed to make their decisions."[7]

There are those who think lobbyists make it difficult for legislators to take a disinterested view of impending legislation, not so much because lobbyists hound them in the corridors of the Capitol but because of the insidious influence of lobbyists, an influence they have acquired because of the campaign contributions they—or, rather, their clients—make. One month after the 1982 congressional elections, Elizabeth Drew wrote that "the role that money is currently playing in American politics is different both in scope and in nature from anything that has gone before." And she argued that "the result of all this is that . . . the ability of even the best of the legislators to focus on broad questions, to act independently, or to lead has been seriously impaired."[8] The *Washington Post* reported in 1981 that the oil industry had doubled its contributions between 1978 and 1980. "One of the nation's largest and wealthiest industries had begun to exert itself as an agent for change in American politics." And the *Post* pointed out that "among the 103 GOP freshmen receiving significant contributions last year, only two voted against the industry on a close 49–47 vote not to table an oil amendment to the tax bill. . . ."[9]

Like other industries, the oil industry channels its contributions to congressmen through political action committees, the so-called PACs. According to the *Post,* there are ninety-four oil-industry PACs. There are, of course, many other PACs, and current estimates run as high as 3,300. Fred Wertheimer of Common Cause said in 1982 that there are about 1,300 corporate PACs. Common Cause inveighs without letup against the growth of PACs. Wertheimer warns, "The influence of special-interest groups exerted through their powerful, well-financed and ever-growing political action committees (PACs)—those wealthy campaign-financing arms of corporations, trade and union groups—threaten to overwhelm us all."[10] PACs may not overwhelm us all, but many observers agree with Common Cause that PACs exert a certain amount of pressure on a congressman to support legislation favored by PACs that have contributed to his campaign. As Justin Dart, the president of Dart Industries, the third largest corporate PAC in 1978, said: Dialogue with politicians "is a fine thing but with a little money they hear you better." Or as a reporter for the *Wall Street Journal* put it: "The bulk of special interest contributions represents a sort of investment in the careers of incumbent congressmen and senators with the aim of enhancing the influence of the financing groups. Obviously this money is given to buy influence."[11]

Congressmen themselves worry about the influence of PACs. According to Rep. Timothy E. Wirth of Colorado, "People are beginning to believe that Congress is for sale." And Rep. Michael L. Synar of Oklahoma forecasts that "outside of the three big issues—energy, the economy and government regulation—the major issue of the 80's will be the impact of special interests on this country. They have become such a dominant force in politics. . . ."[12]

How seriously should we take complaints from congressmen about the power of special interests, through the mechanism of PACs, to influence the legislative process? To some degree, when congressmen complain about special interests they are being shrewd politicians—proclaiming to their constituency that, unlike other politicians, they are not under the sway of special interests. Yet, congressmen do seem truly worried about special interests—worried because their need for large amounts of money to run for reelection makes them dependent upon PACs; in 1982, the average cost was expected to be $400,000 for the House and about $1 million for the Senate. But only those who are rich enough to tap their own resources can forswear PACs, because although the campaign finance laws enacted in the mid-1970s and a subsequent Supreme Court ruling established limits of $1,000 for personal contributions and $5,000 for PAC contributions, there is no limit with regard to what the candidate takes out of his own pocket.

The $5,000 limit on contributions from a PAC appears not to give a particular PAC much leverage with a congressman, but PACs run in packs, as the *Post's* report on the oil industry made clear. Moreover, there is no limit to independent expenditures, that is, expenditures that are not directly connected with a candidate's campaign. The *Wall Street Journal* reported in 1982 that "in 1980 the Realtors Political Action Committee allotted about $100,000 for 'independent expenditures' to run campaigns against its enemies rather than help its friends. The effort was so successful that RPAC thinks its independent-expenditures budget may soar as high as $500,000 this year."[13]

It is not only the money of PACs that has made special interests more powerful. According to Edward C. Banfield, the decline of the two main parties "opened new opportunities for the exercise of influence by special interest groups." Other observers point to the congressional reforms of the mid-1970s, which weakened the power of committee chairmen, as a factor causing the growing influence of special interest groups. Without a strong party to provide financial support and without strong committee chairmen to give direction, congressmen are more or less on their own, easily intimidated by special interest groups, who may threaten to withdraw campaign contributions—or even to run negative campaign advertisements—if the congressmen do not vote "right." Representative Synar explains: "They want me to fear my constituents. But it's very difficult to get any consistency in government if everyone is afraid of his constituency. You can't legislate out of fear."[14]

Are those who express such concerns unduly alarmist? Thomas E. Mann argues that it "is easy to overemphasize recent developments at the expense of more stable elements that continue to determine the basic shape of the political process."[15] Nevertheless, not a month goes by without some hand-wringing by a journalist, congressman, or political scientist over the effect special interest groups may be having on the course of government. Speaking of the "American regime's crisis," Walter Dean Burnham fears that a political system cannot "survive very long if every possible interest became organized and moved into the political arena with the aim of realizing its specific objectives and blocking everyone else's."[16]

What is to be done? Some Americans, notably those on the Left, call for a "long revolution, aimed at deconstituting the present structure of power,"[17] but most Americans are wary of radical change. Many, however, are vaguely in favor of measures that may further weaken Congress as an institution—measures of "direct democracy," such as referendums, initiatives—and also in favor of constitutional amendments that, in effect, would tie the hands of Congress, preventing it from deliberating about certain issues. Those who recommend such measures usually are not so much opposed to representative government as suspicious of it, suspicious of its ability to work for the welfare of all Americans because so many congressmen are beholden to special interests.

Although there has been an increasing number of referendums and initiatives throughout the nation, there has been no groundswell of support for direct democracy. There have, however, been many proposals to reform the campaign finance laws in order to weaken—or eliminate—the influence of special interests. Campaign finance is an intricate question, and there are some basic disagreements about what the prescriptions should be, disagreements in the main that are the result of different diagnoses of the disease. Some observers think special interests are too powerful because of too much reform in the 1970s; others think special interests are too powerful because there has been too little reform. Those who think there has not been enough reform usually call for eliminating PACs altogether by having congressional races publicly financed. In their view, money undermines the political process, not necessarily because it corrupts politicians but because it taints the process itself. According to Fred Wertheimer, "We are dealing not only with the actuality of abuse by public officials but with the appearance as well." Wertheimer, moreover, says, "The PACs stand out as one of the major causes of the growing fragmentation of our political system and also of the increasing difficulty we experience in our attempts to reach national consensus. They are a key factor in the growth in America of the special-interest state."[18]

By contrast, those who think there has been too much reform usually call for more PACs, not fewer, so that no one PAC or group of PACs can be very influential. According to Michael Malbin, "*Increasing* the amount of money in politics decreases the power of individual interest groups, while restricting money would be likely to increase the power of those groups organizationally able to take advantage of the situation. Thus, paradoxically, the way to decrease the power of special interests may well be to let them flower."[19] He calls for more private money being expended on campaigns, not less, and would like ceilings raised on contributions.

In sum, in the debate about the power of special interests, there are—broadly speaking—two camps, and each can marshal strong arguments in support of its position. Those who question current limits on campaign contributions and oppose public financing of congressional campaigns argue that the limits "exclude people from participating in the political process and, therefore, prevent them from exercising freedom of speech." They also argue that the limits have resulted in a "bizarre situation that magnifies exponentially the advantage of the wealthy candidate" because he can draw from his own resources. Finally, they charge that public financing would be "a government guaranteed job program for campaign consultants."[20]

By contrast, those who want to reduce or eliminate private money from congressional campaigns argue that the current situation taints the political process, appearing to favor those—like the oil industry—that can afford both to dole out contributions to a large number of candidates and (perhaps even more important) to mount expensive independent-expenditures operations against incumbents they dislike. On the power of the oil industry PACs, a Democratic member of the House commented, "They have virtually unlimited resources, and money counts in elections. I would not look on this as anything but an adverse development." The advocates for more reform also cite the Supreme Court's opinion when it upheld the constitutionality of contribution limits: "To the extent that large contributions are given to secure political quid pro quos from current and potential office holders, the integrity of our system of representative democracy is undermined."[21]

But if some observers worry that without more reform the integrity of representative government will be undermined, others worry that the attempt to eliminate the influence of special interests goes against the kind of representative government the framers of the Constitution intended: an extended commercial republic in which, as Michael Malbin puts it, "diverse economic interests would flourish and compete with each other," attempting to use politics to achieve private economic ends. *The Federalist,* Malbin argues, endorses special interests, for it implies that the more they flourish the less likely it is that any one special interest will predominate. In short, the authors of *The Federalist* did not grudgingly acknowledge the inevitability of special interests; they regarded them as essential to the health of the Republic. Or, as Malbin says, they thought that "nothing is as important in our constitutional scheme of things as the preservation of a system in which a multiplicity of factions flourishes."[22]

Yet, how relevant is *The Federalist,* which Malbin and others continually cite to support their position, to our present discontents? After all, it was written some two hundred years ago, when the United States was a small coastal and predominantly agrarian country of approximately four million people, whereas it is now a large continental and highly industrialized global superpower of more than 225 million people. Would not the authors of *The Federalist* themselves regard their prescriptions as out of date? And would they not be appalled by the current political climate, where PACs spend millions to influence the legislative process? Moreover, how important is the argument of *The Federalist?* Although many scholars regard it as a work of profound political philosophy, it was a hastily written tract composed by three hands—James Madison, Alexander Hamilton, and John Jay—to persuade the delegates to the state ratifying conventions to adopt the Constitution. Finally, why should we assume that the wisdom of *The Federalist* is essential to an understanding of the workings of the American Republic? Some observers argue that *The Federalist* betrays the republican vision implicit in the Declaration of Independence, that it is an argument in favor of a constitution that enabled an undemocratic commercial elite to impose its will on the public because the elite felt, as Lawrence Goodwyn says, that "the democratic polity could not be trusted."[23]

However we regard *The Federalist,* one thing is clear: It is where we must begin in order to examine the problem of special interests in American politics, for *The Federalist* examines the relation between special interests and the public interest. Moreover, for the past seventy years its meaning and relevance have been debated by historians and political scientists. Thus, the first half of this extended essay on special interests will focus on *The Federalist;* the second half will attempt to gauge the influence special interests have had on national politics. But to understand *The Federalist* fully, we need to have some idea of where the notion of interest stood in eighteenth-century Britain and the United States.

Notes

1. *Washington Post,* 15 January 1981, p. A7; ibid., 21 January 1981, p. A34; *Newsweek,* 6 November 1978, p. 50; *Washington Post,* 8 December 1980, p. A3.
2. Cited, Gordon Wood, *The Creation of the American Republic, 1776–1787* (New York: W. W. Norton, 1972), p. 421.
3. *International Herald Tribune,* 10 February 1983, p. 3; cited, John Charles Daly, *The State of the Congress: Can It Meet Tomorrow's Challenges?* (Washington, D.C.: American Enterprise Institute, 1981), p. 1; Edmund Burke, "Speech on Conciliation with the Colonies," in *Edmund Burke: Selected Works,* ed. W. J. Bate (New York: Random House, 1960), p. 128.
4. Cited, Daly, *State of the Congress,* pp. 1–2.
5. Jonathan Raban, *Old Glory: An American Voyage* (New York: Simon & Schuster, 1981), p. 110.
6. Daly, *State of the Congress,* p. 16. See also Millicent Fenwick, "In Congress: Buy Your Seat or Sell Your Vote," *Washington Post,* 9 November 1982, p. 21.
7. *New York Times,* 25 July 1982, p. E5; ibid.
8. Elizabeth Drew, "Politics and Money," *New Yorker* 6 December 1982, p. 54.
9. *Washington Post,* 15 September 1981, p. A2.
10. Fund-raising letter received by author from Common Cause, June 1982.
11. Dart's remark and article in *Wall Street Journal* cited by Fred Wertheimer, "Commentaries" in *Parties, Interest Groups, and Campaign Finance Laws,* ed. Michael J. Malbin (Washington, D.C.: American Enterprise Institute, 1980), p. 194.
12. *New York Times,* 25 July 1982, p. E5; ibid., 11 January 1980, p. 16.
13. *Wall Street Journal,* 1 August 1982, p. 1.
14. Edward C. Banfield, "Party 'Reform' in Retrospect," in *Political Parties in the Eighties,* ed. Robert A. Goldwin (Washington, D.C.: American Enterprise Institute, 1980), p. 28; *New York Times,* 11 January 1980, p. 16.
15. Thomas E. Mann, "Election and Change in Congress," in *The New Congress,* ed. Thomas E. Mann and Norman J. Ornstein (Washington, D.C.: American Enterprise Institute, 1981), p. 52.
16. Walter Dean Burnham, "The Constitution, Capitalism, and the Need for Rationalized Regulation," in *How Capitalistic Is the Constitution?,* ed. Robert A. Goldwin and William A. Schambra (Washington, D.C.: American Enterprise Institute, 1982), pp. 103, 95.
17. "The People's Two Bodies," *Democracy* 1 (1981):24.
18. Wertheimer, "Commentaries," pp. 196, 199.
19. Ibid., p. 184.
20. David W. Adamany, "Discussion," in Malbin, *Parties, Interest Groups, and Campaign Finance Laws,* p. 223; Walter Shapiro, "And the Rich, More and More, Shall Inherit Congress," *Washington Post,* 11 July 1982, p. C2.
21. *Washington Post,* 15 September 1981, p. A2; cited, Wertheimer, p. 196.
22. Ibid., p. 216.
23. Lawrence Goodwyn, "Organizing Democracy: The Limits of Theory and Practice," *Democracy* 1 (1981):57.

PART I

TOWARD A SCIENCE OF POLITICS

The spirit of liberty is the spirit which is not too sure it is right.

—Learned Hand

One is afraid to think of all that the genus "patriot" embraces.

—George Eliot

1

Patriots and Scientists

When Samuel Johnson thundered to Boswell in 1775 that "patriotism is the last refuge of a scoundrel," he was not thinking of American patriots, though he disliked their pleas for liberty when they themselves were slave-holders. Nor was he thinking of those who profess a love of their country and a willingness to take up arms in defense of it. He was attacking, rather, a particular approach to politics that he thought dishonest and irresponsible, and the man he probably had in mind when he uttered the word "scoundrel" was John Wilkes. Wilkes's exclusion from Parliament in 1769 had resulted in many riots, ceaseless public meetings, and innumerable petitions to the king. The supporters of Wilkes, who often called themselves Patriots, said that there was an "alarming crisis" at hand. Johnson emphatically disagreed. If an alarming crisis were to arise, Johnson said in "The False Alarm" (1770), it would be the fault of "patriots" who were raising false alarms about the ministry in power, making "general accusations of indeterminate wickedness, and obscure hints of impossible designs." Such wild charges fire the people "with the fever of epidemic patriotism," so that they "see a thousand evils, though they cannot show them, and grow impatient for a remedy, though they know not what."[1]

The patriotism Johnson was attacking was less a coherent body of thought than a mixed bag of notions that had first been formulated in the early decades of the eighteenth century by Henry St. John, Viscount Boling-broke, who was the leading opposition figure to the ministry of Robert Walpole as well as a close friend of such writers as Swift, Pope, and Gay. Bolingbroke called Walpole's ministry a cabal that was "drawing the whole wealth of the nation and the whole power of the state to itself." Run by men swayed by private interest, by men who were venal and corrupt, the ministry had tainted all of English life, so that "the spirit of private interest prevails among us." According to Bolingbroke, the only remedy for a country so sunk in corruption and close to ruin was a Patriot King who would lead his people away from the pursuit of private interest, making

Britain once again a "genuine" polity—one without factions, one in which "the head and all the members are united by one common interest."[2]

Such are the outlines of Bolingbroke's patriotism, a patriotism he preached in *The Craftsman,* a semiweekly that appeared from 1726 to 1736, *A Dissertation Upon Parties* (1734), *Letter on the Spirit of Patriotism* (1736), and *The Idea of a Patriot King* (1749). Bolingbroke was a Tory, a defender of the landed aristocracy; only men of property, he said, were capable having a disinterested view of the common good because only they were truly independent, free from commercial attachments. Yet his patriotism had much in common with the patriotism of the radical Whigs, who stood at the opposite end of the political spectrum. As Bolingbroke said of Cato, the pen name of John Trenchard and Thomas Gordon, the radical Whigs who published the journal *Cato's Letters:* "The object of our complaint is the same, as well as our principles in political affairs. Where he left off I began . . . against the mischievous consequences of venality and corruption." Both Bolingbroke and the radical Whigs agreed that money, as Bolingbroke said, had become the very "rule and sinew of government." And both Bolingbroke and the radical Whigs agreed that, as Trenchard and Gordon said, Walpole's "wicked and desperate ministers" were enacting measures that would "ruin and enslave their Country."[3]

The chief characteristic of patriotism—whether of the Tory or the radical Whig variety—was a preoccupation with governmental corruption. In the eighteenth century, corruption had a specific meaning in addition to its general one. It alluded to the influence of the crown, the crown's ability to secure by various means (such as dispensing offices) enough support in Parliament for the measures it wanted enacted. Many writers supported corruption in this specific sense and argued, as did David Hume, that "some degree and some kind of it are . . . necessary to the preservation of our mixed government." Bolingbroke, however, thought that the crown's influence was subverting the British Constitution. Pope's epic, *The Dunciad,* is in great part an elaborate satire on the corruption endemic in Walpole's administration. In Book Four Pope personifies Interest as a creature who flings her "gay livery"—the costume worn by retainers and servants—on people. Under Walpole, that is, the country had become rife with craven people who thought only of advancing their private interests. Interest, by which Pope means private interest, goes hand in hand with corruption, with the result that in the "dull and venal" world of Walpole's England, "drowned was sense, and shame, and right, and wrong. . . ."[4]

But if for Bolingbroke and Pope "interest" was a term of abuse, for many—perhaps most—Englishmen it was a more neutral term, the term of an age in which "interest itself . . . could be advanced as the self-justifying rationale of *all* political conduct. . . ."[5] The term had first come into use in England through the work of the Duc de Rohan, a Huguenot statesman whose *Treatise on the Interests of the Princes and States of Christendom* was translated into English in 1640. According to the Duc de Rohan, the process of considering one's interest is a legitimate and rational enterprise, one similar to the process Descartes describes in *Discourse on Method* (1637). Just as Descartes's method is supposed to lead to the rejection of all ideas that are not clear and distinct, Rohan's method would enable a prince to gain a clear and distinct idea of his political situation. The passions, as Rohan makes clear, have no role to play in this process: "In matters of state one must not let oneself be guided . . . by violent passions, which agitate us in various ways as soon as they possess us . . . but by our own interest guided by reason alone. . . ." Rohan implies that the prince's very attempt to consult his interest enables him to control his passions better, so that eventually he will truly understand his political situation. "Interest alone will never lie."[6]

Entering the language as a term connected with statecraft, interest was generally associated with the conduct of foreign affairs, and the latter half of the seventeenth century saw the publication of numerous pamphlets on "the interest of England." Yet if, as Rohan said, interest never lies, it was inevitable that the notion would be grasped by those who wanted to define their own interest vis-à-vis the prince's. "Fortified by the new respectibility of proclaiming one's 'interest,' people argued that each man's legitimate concern for his own safety and property was the proper starting-point for any search for the public good." In 1647, King Charles acknowledged the new political realities: Whereas he had previously spoken only of the common good, he now spoke of the "satisfaction of all interests." By the second half of the century, " 'interest' had become the accepted framework of political discussion."[7]

Nevertheless, some writers regarded the notion of interest with suspicion because they were unsure of what it meant. On the one hand, it seemed to signify the just rights of certain groups in the polity; on the other hand, it seemed to signify the pursuit of financial gain to the detriment of the common good. In the following passage, a mid-seventeenth-century writer argues that all claims of interest are not necessarily claims in behalf of a narrow self-interest: "Whatever it is that a man hath interest in, if that interest (as he conceives at least) be a just interest, shall he not have liberty to plead for it. . . . Must he pass for a covetous worldling, a self seeker, a lover of his profit . . . because he asks for his own?"[8] The writer is defensive because he knows that the vagueness of "interest" makes it a potentially dangerous word to invoke: one man's just "public" interest is another man's unjust "private" interest.

Thomas Hobbes thought the attempt on the part of different interests in the polity to agree upon which interests were just was bound to fail, not because man is avaricious but because he is dogmatic—inclined not to accept another person's version of what is a just interest. "In reasoning," Hobbes says in *Leviathan* (1651), "a man must take heed of words; which besides the signification of what we imagine of their nature, have a significa- tion also of the nature, disposition, and interest of the speaker; . . . for one man calleth *wisdom,* what another calleth *fear;* and one *cruelty,* what anoth- er *justice.* . . ."[9] "Interest" is an open-ended word, one whose content, so to speak, lends itself to being shaped by the nature, disposition, and, indeed, interest of the speaker. If disputes about interests were allowed free rein the polity would be torn apart by rival factions, each claiming it alone knows what a just interest is. Hobbes believed that if most men would reason according to scientific principles—something he thought possible but un- likely—they would realize that their "true interest" lies in agreeing to be ruled by an absolute monarch, for all interests except man's "true interest" in achieving a secure and tranquil existence are divisive forces. In *Human Nature* Hobbes describes two kinds of learning:

> From the principal parts of Nature, Reason and Passion, have proceeded two kinds of learning, mathematical and *dogmatical:* the former is free from controversy and dispute, because it consisteth in comparing figure and motion only; in which things, truth, and *the interest of men,* oppose not each other: but in the other there is *nothing indisputable, because it compareth men,* and meddleth with *their right and profit; in which, as oft as reason is against a man,* so oft will a man be against reason.[10]

Only an absolute monarch, by force of his authority, can resolve the endless controversy engendered by "the interest of men."

Hobbes's skepticism about the possibility of arriving at an agreement about just interests was similar to the skepticism of his French contempo- raries, Pascal and La Rochefoucauld, who both attacked notions of interest that were indebted to Cartesian rationalism. According to La Ro- chefoucauld, the act of considering one's interest is not as easy as Cartesian rationalists make it out to be, for man is a creature who is obscure even to himself. "It is easy to deceive ourselves without knowing it as it is hard to deceive others without their finding it out." And because man finds it difficult if not impossible to clarify his own interests, it is highly unlikely that he can disentangle just interests from unjust ones. "Self-interest speaks all sorts of languages and plays all sorts of roles," La Rochefoucauld says, "even that of disinterestedness."[11] Although interest governs the world, interest itself is a mysterious and opaque force.

The English political theorists who favored republican government were not affected by the skepticism of either La Rochefoucauld or Hobbes. If, according to Hobbes, self-interest should make one a supporter of absolute monarchy, according to James Harrington, self-interest should make one support a commonwealth that recognizes "true and real interests." Yet in *Oceana* (1656), Harrington finds it difficult to clarify what he means by "true and real interests." Sometimes he castigates the "mire" of private interest, sometimes he suggests that the pursuit of private interest is acceptable provided it is done in a way consonant with "the common interest." As he says, "To take up that which regards the common good or interest; all this is to no more end, than to persuade every man in a popular government not to carve of himself of that which he desires most but to be more mannerly at the public table. . . ."[12] Acting "mannerly" seems to mean acting both privately and publicly, acting both as a self-interested man who wants food but also as a disinterested citizen who realizes that eating is a civil occasion that requires certain forms of conduct if anarchy is not to prevail. How one decides who is acting mannerly and who is not is never clarified.

By the end of the seventeenth century the mainstream of English political writing supported a modified version of Harrington's limited justification of private interests, modified in the sense that most political writers were not supporters of republican government. George Savile, the Duke of Halifax, thought that a responsible statesman was someone—like himself—who balanced different interests in order to keep the state on an even keel. Such a political actor is what Halifax calls a trimmer. According to Halifax's *The Character of a Trimmer* (1688), men of civic virtue do not so much speak for different interests as find ways of reconciling them in the greater interest of the stability of the state.

Halifax does not agonize over the distinction between just and unjust interests. He accepts the legitimacy of all interests but regards the trimmer as essential for making sure that these interests act mannerly. Like Hobbes, Halifax is skeptical of man's ability to understand his true interest, less because men are dogmatic, as Hobbes said, than because they usually have myopic views of the world and cannot see wherein their true long-range interest lies. "If men," Halifax says, "must be supposed always to follow their true interest, it must be meant of a new manufactory of mankind by God Almighty; there must be some new clay, the old stuff never yet made any such infallible creature."[13] Only statesmen are in a position to know best about what is in the true interest of most people, not because statesmen can better fathom the motives of people but because statesmen are in the best position to know what the state requires if it is to remain strong and stable.

Balancing—and indeed controlling—different interests, Halifax's trimmer bears some resemblance to Hobbes's monarch, who resolves all disputes. Moreover, Halifax accepts Hobbes's notion that the true interest of most people is in attaining a secure and tranquil existence. But Halifax thought absolute monarchy bred civil discontent, not security and tranquillity, and he supported the Act of Rights (1689), which limited the sovereignty of the king. This act became the foundation of the so-called mixed constitution of Britain, which consisted of three equal estates: King, Lords, and Commons. For Halifax, the British Constitution was a noble middle way, an embodiment of the trimmer's instincts in that it avoided the extremes of monarchy and commonwealth—avoided both "devouring prerogative and licentious freedom." "True virtue hath ever been thought a trimmer, dwelling in the middle between the two extremes."[14]

By the middle of the eighteenth century, most Englishmen had adopted the trimmer's notion of virtue, scorning both those who advocated a republican commonwealth and those who yearned for a return of the old monarchy of the Stuarts. It was taken for granted by most political writers that politicians spoke for different "interests": the court interest, country interest, landed interest, city interest, moneyed interest, merchant interest, mercantile interest. And it was the job of statesmen, as Halifax said, to "balance" interests just as the captain of a small boat would balance its weight. "The innocent word Trimmer signifieth no more than this, that if Men are together in a Boat, and one part of the Company would weigh it down on one side, another would make it lean as much to the contrary; it happeneth there is a third Opinion of those, who conceive it would do as well, if the Boat went even, without endangering the passengers. . . ."[15]

According to Halifax, the statesman, like Bolingbroke's Patriot, would be concerned with the public interest—that is, with the general welfare of the country—but Halifax assumed that disinterested statesmen must take into account, if not necessarily accept, the claims of all the different private interests. Bolingbroke, however, rejected the idea that different private interests were inevitable. Or so he said, for by the middle of the eighteenth century most Englishmen probably regarded Bolingbroke's patriotic rhetoric with weariness and cynicism (Bolingbroke died in 1751). Yet such rhetoric could still be used to powerful effect, and some writers thought it truly pernicious insofar as it inflamed public opinion, supposedly promoting civil disorder. A year before Samuel Johnson startled Boswell by speaking in such a "strong determined tone" on the subject of patriotism, he published "The Patriot" (1774), in which he explains more fully why he intensely disliked those who called themselves patriots. "A man sometimes starts up a Patriot, only by disseminating discontent and propagating reports of secret influence, of dangerous counsels, of violated rights and encroaching usurpation."[16] According to Johnson, a patriot is a demagogue who stirs up popular feeling against the government by concocting absurd charges.

Johnson's essay, however, suffers from being riddled with the very language of accusation that he criticizes. Like Bolingbroke, he focuses on men, not measures. And, like Bolingbroke, he attacks the character of those with whom he disagrees. He concludes "The Patriot" with a scathing attack on those "who, by deceiving the credulous with fictitious mischiefs, overbearing the weak by audacity of falsehood, by appealing to the judgment of ignorance, and flattering the vanity of meanness, by slandering honesty and insulting dignity, have gathered round them whatever the kingdom can supply of base, and gross, and profligate; and 'raised by merit to this bad eminence,' arrogate to themselves the name of *Patriots.*"[17] Johnson's essay seems more like a symptom of the disease of patriotism than a remedy.

"The Patriot," moreover, founders on a distinction Johnson makes between true and false patriots: A true patriot "is always ready to countenance the just claims and animate the reasonable hopes of the people."[18] Many Englishmen, however, considered the claims of Wilkes and his followers to be eminently just, yet Johnson dismisses the supporter of Wilkes as a false Patriot—someone whose "design in all his declamation is not to benefit his country, but to gratify his malice"[19]—dismisses him, that is, as someone motivated by private interest, not an interest in making money but an interest in assuaging his envy and resentment. Johnson himself, however, was accused of acting out of interest, of taking the court's side on many questions because he had accepted a pension from the king. Who was acting out of self-interest and who was the disinterested patriot? Johnson's essay does not clarify the question Harrington had wrestled with more than one hundred years earlier: how to distinguish "true and real interests" from the "mire" of private interest.

About twenty-five years before Johnson wrote "The Patriot," David Hume complained about "the zeal of *patriots.*" But Hume, who thought Bolingbroke's arguments defective in "method, and precision,"[20] does not try to distinguish "true and real" or "just" interests from the mire of private interest. Instead, he argues that it is foolish to assume that any one group is a spokesman for the country's "true and real" interests. According to Hume, different opinions concerning the Constitution inevitably arise "even among persons of the best understanding," and therefore it is wrong to accuse one's political opponents of subverting the Constitution. Such polemical excesses result in "extraordinary ferment" and fill the nation with "violent animosities." "Would men be moderate and consistent," Hume says, "their claims might be admitted, at least might be examined."[21]

Hume was not simply making a plea for moderation in political discourse. He was arguing that the language of the Patriots was anachronistic, not in accord with the realities of a society in which commercial expansion has bred different interest groups. When Hume says that there are "zealots on both sides who kindle up the passions of their partisans and, under pretense of public good, pursue the interests and ends of their particular factions,"22 he is *not* concerned that such factions exist but that each pretends to speak for the public good. Such a posture of disinterest is the merest pretense; each faction is concerned mainly with advancing its own interests. Hume is not trying to unmask the factions, not trying to say—as Johnson would—that they are dishonest. Rather, he is trying to persuade them to unmask themselves—to admit that they are based on interest rather than on what he calls principle. Hume thinks that if factions admit that they are pursuing their own interests, they are more likely to be accommodating, more likely to seek compromise. Acknowledging the reality of private interest instead of trying to banish private interest from the polity would make factions less given to considering each other wholly malign, and therefore the chances of violent civil discord would be reduced.

The central distinction that informs Hume's political essays is that between "parties from principle" and "parties from interest" (Hume uses the words "parties" and "factions" interchangeably): "Parties from *principle,* especially abstract speculative principle, are known only to modern times and are, perhaps, the most extraordinary and unaccountable phenomenon that has yet appeared in human affairs."23 Hume was thinking primarily of the different religious "parties" that had arisen not only in Britain but throughout Europe in the seventeenth century, parties that had differed with one another on the grounds of religious principle. The growth of such parties led very often to violent animosity, even civil war, and when Hobbes warns of the dangers of faction he is primarily referring to factions based on religious differences. Hume, however, acknowledges that such parties no longer exist. What Hume is saying is that the contemporary parties from principle are really parties from interest—parties whose differences are basically economic in nature—*only they do not say so.* If these parties would only acknowledge that they are, in fact, parties from interest, then English political debate would become more moderate because parties from interest "are the most reasonable and the most excusable."24

Hume, then, may be said to have offered a solution to the problem of distinguishing "true and real" interests from the mire of private interest. Like Hobbes, he thinks it is virtually impossible for men to come to any agreement about what is a true or just interest. He does not think, however, that an absolute monarch is necessary to resolve such questions. There is no need, Hume implies, to resort to Hobbes's drastic solution because parties from interest, which are the most common factions in predominantly commercial societies, are capable of arriving at compromises in which the claims of each party are partially heeded. In effect, Hume is asking each faction to give up its claim to speak for the "true interest" of England; once this is done, then the spokesmen of the factions can move toward a legislative compromise in which no one faction is completely neglected.

But Hume does not assert only that factions are inevitable in predominantly commercial societies and therefore should be allowed to exist because they generally are not dangerous. "To abolish all distinctions of party," he says, is impracticable and not even "desirable in a free government."[25] The factions commerce breeds are essential, Hume implies, to the workings of a free society. The more a polity's citizens are wedded to commerce, the more likely they are to be strong proponents of liberty. "But where luxury nourishes commerce and industry, the peasants, by a proper cultivation of the land, become rich and independent; while the tradesmen and merchants acquire a share of the property and draw authority and consideration to that *middling rank of men who are the best and firmest basis of public liberty*" (emphasis added).[26] The new commercial factions, Hume argues, "covet equal laws, which may secure their property and preserve them from monarchical as well as aristocratical tyranny."

Hume was not the first to make a case for the legitimacy of parties from interest—or what we would call special interests. He acknowledged his debt to Bernard Mandeville, whom he praised as one of a number of writers "who have begun to put the science of man on a new footing. . . ."[27] What connects Hume with Mandeville, however, is not only their praise of commerce and private interest but also their belief that they were looking at politics from a "scientific" point of view. In the eighteenth century, science referred not to what we call the sciences but to any uniform body of knowledge. The eighteenth-century "scientists of politics," who include Mandeville, Hume, Montesquieu, and Adam Smith, took their model from biology rather than mathematics. They were less interested in deducing the nature of justice than in arriving at some general "laws" of politics by looking at the kinds of polities that have existed. All the eighteenth-century scientists of politics were well versed in history.

We can discern, then, two strains in eighteenth-century political thought: the patriotic and the scientific. Yet, labeling writers in this way can be misleading. In "The Patriot," Samuel Johnson sounds very much like Bolingbroke, but he also subscribed to the science of politics. "Causeless discontent and seditious violence," he says in "The False Alarm," "will grow less frequent, and less formidable, as the science of government is better ascertained by a diligent study of the theory of man."[28] Johnson detested Hume's lack of religion, but agreed with him that the expansion of commerce was good for society—not simply because it reduced the likelihood of violent factions but also because it enabled the poor to better their condition. Both Hume and Johnson are called Tories, but their approach to politics does not resemble Bolingbroke's, and Bolingbroke is also called a Tory. Bolingbroke's politics is the politics of nostalgia; he looks to the past rather than to the future, and he regards the predominance of commercial men as bad for the health of Britain. By and large, Patriots were distrustful of commerce, but perhaps the most important distinction between the Patriots and the "scientists" is that the former thought factions could be avoided by urging everyone to consider, as Bolingbroke said, "the good of his country," whereas the latter came to the conclusion that in predominantly commercial societies factions—that is, special interests—were inevitable and could be destroyed only by destroying liberty.

Thus, if Patriots attacked private interest and looked upon commerce with suspicion, scientists recognized the legitimacy of different private interests and argued that the rise of commerce fostered liberty and civic order because factions based on economic concerns—what Hume calls "parties from interest"—tend to be more capable of seeking compromise than factions based upon principle. As Adam Smith—Hume's disciple and friend—says, "The good temper and moderation of contending factions seems to be the most essential circumstance in the public morals of a free people"; and commerce fosters such good-tempered factions. Of Europe after the fall of the Roman Empire, Smith writes in *The Wealth of Nations:* "Commerce and manufactures gradually introduced order and good government, and with them, the liberty and security of individuals, among the inhabitants of the country, who had before lived almost in a continual state of war with their neighbors, and of servile dependency upon their superiors. This, though it has been the least observed, is by far the most important of all their effects. Mr. Hume is the only writer who, so far as I know, has hitherto taken notice of it."[29] Smith is not quite right, for Johnson had also taken note of the moderating effects of commerce; many of his essays praise the industry of commercial man while pointing out that idleness breeds strong and dangerous passions that are difficult to control.

Proponents of a science of politics never suggested that Britain should be run by commercial men. Disinterested statesmen—men of enlightened opinions and extensive views—were necessary not only to foster commerce but also to find ways of mitigating some of its harmful effects. Indeed, in *The Wealth of Nations* Smith addresses his arguments to disinterested legislators, trying to keep them from being swayed by the protectionist schemes of merchants and manufacturers. Few scientists were as enthusiastic about commerce as Bernard Mandeville, who argued that the "private vices" of commerce result in "public benefits." Most of the scientists thought Mandeville went too far in his witty deflation of Bolingbrokian humbug. Surely some vices, Johnson said to Boswell, are harmful to society. If everyone lies, then society will dissolve, because "society is held together by communication and information. . . ." And Hume spoke of the need to have public-spirited men who would restrain "the avarice and ambition of particular men." Even Mandeville acknowledged that "dextrous politicians"—men, supposedly, like Halifax's trimmer—are needed to transform by "skillful management" private vices into public benefits.[30]

Mandeville, Hume, Johnson, and Smith, then, did not abandon the notion of public-spiritedness or civic virtue; they certainly did not think that all would be well in Britain if commercial men were allowed to do as they pleased. Even Smith thought that government had many important functions to perform, and therefore the country needed wise and public-spirited legislators, men who would be in favor of commercial expansion but not see things only from a commercial point of view. Hume and other scientists were not opposed to public-spiritedness; they were opposed to a public-spiritedness that was hostile to commerce, a public-spiritedness that was self-righteous and opposed to deliberation, a public-spiritedness that manifested itself in the assumption that disagreements occur only if men are venal and corrupt. Perhaps, as Johnson claimed, the Patriots' professions of disinterest were disingenuous. But for Hume and other scientists, it was important to stop speculating about motives—stop speculating about who was truly disinterested and who was acting out of private interest—for Hume thought that when politicians stand, as it were, on their disinterest, deliberation about what is in the public interest becomes virtually impossible. The politics of disinterest leaves no room for disagreement about what is in the public interest—leaves no room, that is, for deliberation, because disagreement is seen as a sign of corruption. More than any other scientist, Hume realized that a concern with the motives of men rather than with their measures abets civil discord because it makes deliberation about public policy impossible.

Perhaps the main difference between the Patriot and the scientist was the former's confidence in the ability of disinterested men to reach agreement on matters of public policy. The scientist was much less sanguine, for he had much less faith in man's ability to reason clearly, either about the public interest or even about his own interest. Descendants of La Rochefoucauld and Hobbes, scientists doubted whether a body of disinterested men would all arrive at the same clear and distinct idea of what was in the public interest. Descendants of Descartes and the Duc de Rohan, Patriots were more confident that such an enterprise would succeed, that consensus could be reached.

"It has sometimes been asked," Johnson begins one of his essays in *The Adventurer,* "why men, equally reasonable, and equally lovers of truth, do not always think in the same manner." The formation of opinions, Johnson says, is a very mysterious phenomenon. We are very inconstant in our opinions, inconstant even in our opinions about those questions "wherein we have most interest." If men continually change their minds about what is in their own interest—"we see a little, and form an opinion; we see more and change it"—then it is understandable why they disagree so often about the public interest. The "inconstancy and unsteadiness" of opinion, Johnson says, is such that it "ought certainly to teach us moderation and forbearance towards those, who cannot accommodate themselves to our sentiments. . . ."[31]

Hume would agree with the need for moderation and forbearance, but he would make the point somewhat differently. Hume distinguishes between opinion and interest: "Though men be much governed by interest, yet even interest itself and all human affairs are entirely governed by *opinion.* "[32] The distinction between opinion and interest is essentially a distinction between ideas that arise out of moral concerns and ideas that arise out of economic concerns. Hume's notion of opinion was strongly influenced by Hobbes, who says that "men, vehemently in love with their own new opinions, though never so absurd, and obstinately bent to maintain them, gave those their opinions . . . [the] reverenced name of conscience. . . ."[33] Opinion, both Hume and Hobbes imply, is a mysterious and dangerous force, one difficult to account for, predict, and control. Hume was more sanguine than Hobbes because he thought the rise of commerce would reduce the likelihood that violent opinions would infect Britain, but Hume was too well versed in the dark realities of history to assume that factions based upon opinion—factions that are dogmatic and potentially violent— would never rise up again.

Hume, unlike Johnson, practiced what he preached: his arguments attacking patriotism were tactful and moderate; Johnson's often were not. But Hume, as John Plamenatz says, "had a habit that is not endearing. It was one of his favorite occupations to point out that other people's quarrels were unnecessary."[34] Hume's reasonability, the reasonability of a man who looks at the world from the comfort of his study, does at times ring hollow. He was inclined to dismiss politics as a world in which zealous factions would always hold sway, but as a man of public spirit he was concerned lest zealous men plunge Britain into civil violence. And, as a man of public spirit, he believed he had to engage in the art of persuasion—trying to convince Patriots that they should, in effect, become scientists. Hume was by temperament a moderate man; Johnson was not. But both passionately defended the British political order, and both thought that patriotism was dangerous to that order. Moderation, Hume says, does not mean that men should "abate the industry and passion with which every individual is bound to pursue the good of his country."[35]

Fearful of civil discord, the scientists sought a rhetoric of accommodation. Fearful that venal men were unbalancing the Constitution, the Patriots preferred a rhetoric that separated men into disinterested citizens who always had the common good in mind and self-interested citizens. Scientists like Hume and Smith—if not Johnson—tried to persuade Patriots to moderate their zeal. But Patriots like Bolingbroke and John Wilkes had no desire to listen to the scientists, for they were certain who was right; those who disagreed with their prescriptions should be denounced as corrupt. For the Patriots, then, the art of persuasion was irrelevant to the political process. On one side were the disinterested citizens who agreed with their position; on the other side was a mass of venal and dishonest persons, animated by private interest. The Patriots, we might say, thought that what we would call special interests were if not illegitimate at least unworthy of being heeded by politicians.

Despite the Patriots' inflammatory rhetoric, things did not fall apart in Britain, in part because patriotic arguments held little appeal for the citizens of a country in which commerce was expanding rapidly. "Who now reads Bolingbroke?" Burke asked in 1790. "Who ever read him through?"[36] Never very influential in Britain, Bolingbroke and the radical Whigs were taken very seriously in the American colonies.[37] The pervasiveness of the patriotic cast of mind was one of the central political problems Madison, Hamilton, and Jay had to address when they composed *The Federalist.*

Notes

1. R. W. Chapman, ed. *Life of Johnson* (London: Oxford University Press, 1970), p. 615; *Samuel Johnson: Political Writings,* ed. Donald J. Greene (New Haven: Yale University Press, 1977), pp. 335–37.
2. Cited, Isaac Kramnick, *Bolingbroke and His Circle: The Politics of Nostalgia in the Age of Walpole* (Cambridge: Harvard University Press, 1968), pp. 73, 79.
3. Cited, Kramnick, *Bolingbroke and His Circle,* p. 248; ibid., p. 73; cited, Bernard Bailyn, *The Origins of American Politics* (New York: Alfred A. Knopf, 1968), p. 44.
4. David Hume, "Of the Independence of Parliament," in *David Hume's Political Essays,* ed. Charles W. Hendel (Indianapolis: Library of Liberal Arts, 1953), p. 70; *Alexander Pope: Selected Poetry,* ed. Martin Price (New York: New American Library, 1970), pp. 297, 300.
5. Felix Raab, *The English Face of Machiavelli* (London: Routledge & Kegan Paul, 1964), p. 248.
6. Cited, J. A. W. Gunn, *Politics and the Public Interest in the Seventeenth Century* (London: Routledge & Kegan Paul, 1969), pp. 36–38. Gunn's discussion of the rise of the term "interest" is invaluable. Also helpful is Albert O. Hirschman, *The Passions and the Interests* (Princeton: Princeton University Press, 1977).
7. Gunn, *Politics and the Public Interest,* p. xi; King Charles cited, ibid., p. 49; Raab, *English Face of Machiavelli,* p. 238.
8. Cited, Gunn, *Politics and the Public Interest,* p. 41.

9. Thomas Hobbes, *Leviathan,* ed. Michael Oakeshott (New York: Macmillan, 1962), p. 40.
10. Cited, Raab, *English Face of Machiavelli,* p. 239n.
11. *The Maxims of La Rochefoucauld,* trans. Louis Kronenberger (New York: Random House, 1959), pp. 54, 40.
12. Cited, Gunn, *Politics and the Public Interest,* pp. 114–15.
13. Cited, Raab, *English Face of Machiavelli,* p. 247.
14. Cited, Kramnick, *Bolingbroke and His Circle,* p. 141.
15. Cited, Harvey Mansfield, *Statesmanship and Party Government: A Study of Burke and Bolingbroke* (Chicago: University of Chicago Press, 1965), p. 241.
16. Greene, *Johnson: Political Writings,* p. 391.
17. Ibid., p. 400.
18. Ibid., p. 394.
19. Ibid., p. 391.
20. Cited, Garry Wills, *Explaining America* (New York: Doubleday, 1981), p. 22.
21. David Hume, "That Politics May Be Reduced to a Science," in Hendel, *Hume's Political Essays,* pp. 21–23.
22. Ibid., p. 20.
23. David Hume, "Of Parties in General," in Hendel, *Hume's Political Essays,* p. 81.
24. Ibid., p. 79.
25. David Hume, "Of the Coalition of Parties," in Hendel, *Hume's Political Essays,* p. 93.
26. David Hume, "Of Refinement in the Arts," in Hendel, *Hume's Political Essays,* pp. 128–29.
27. Cited, Charles W. Hendel, "Introduction," in Hendel, *Hume's Political Essays,* p. xi.
28. Greene, *Johnson: Political Writings,* p. 318.
29. Adam Smith, *The Wealth of Nations,* ed. Edwin Canaan (New York: Random House, 1937), pp. 729, 385.
30. Chapman, *Life of Johnson,* pp. 948–49; Hendel, *Hume's Political Essays,* p. 20; Irwin Primer, ed., *The Fable of the Bees* (New York: Capricorn, 1962), p. 23.
31. *Samuel Johnson: Essays from the Rambler, Adventurer, and Idler,* ed. W. J. Bate (New Haven: Yale University Press, 1968), pp. 250–55.
32. Hume, "Of the British Government," in Hendel, *Hume's Political Essays,* p. 75.
33. Hobbes, *Leviathan,* p. 57.
34. John Plamenatz, *Man and Society,* vol. 1 (London: Longman, 1963), p. 325.
35. Hume, "That Politics May Be Reduced to a Science," in Hendel, *Hume's Political Essays,* p. 21.
36. Edmund Burke, "Reflections on the Revolution in France," in *Edmund Burke on Government, Politics, and Society,* ed. B. W. Hill (New York: International Publications Service, 1970), p. 357.
37. For a discussion of why Bolingbroke's patriotism no longer was a strong force in Britain in the second half of the eighteenth century, see Isaac Kramnick, "Republican Revisionism Revisited," *American Historical Review* 87 (1982):629–64.

2
Patriotism Triumphant, Patriotism Contained

Soreness, Jealousy, Distrust

The patriotic cast of mind flourished in the mid-eighteenth-century American colonies. The colonists were especially addicted to pamphlets and essays that praised true patriots and warned of false patriots. False patriots were often difficult to ferret out, according to the *Boston Evening Post* of 19 May 1755, for many "disguise their designs under a show of public spirit and zeal for the liberties of their country," yet they had to be unmasked. Possessed by "that monster, *the lust of lawless authority,*" false patriots were capable of finding manifold and subtle ways of betraying the public interest. So argued the anonymous author of "The Watchman," a series of essays that laid out, according to a contemporary reader, "the inner workings of conspiracy against the public good."[1]

"The Watchman" is an appropriate title, for it suggests the suspicion with which its author regarded those who ruled him. Like many colonists, he believed that the people had to be vigilant to protect their liberty from being undermined by corrupt politicians. True patriots, he admitted, did exist; they were men who had no "design" on an office, they did not seek to use it for their private interest. Financially independent, true patriots could not be bought or meanly influenced. But the author of "The Watchman" did not believe that there were many true patriots, for his essays dwell on "the artifices by which the villains of the political world, both small and great, generally mislead the easy multitude who entrust them with power."[2] Such deceptions, he implied, are commonplace.

The fears rehearsed in "The Watchman" were by no means atypical. They appeared in pamphlets and newspapers from Massachusetts to South Carolina. By the 1750s, in fact, a generation of colonists had been nourished on writings that often were filled with long quotations from Bolingbroke and the radical Whigs. "More than any other single group of writers,"

Bernard Bailyn says, "they shaped the mind of the American revolutionary generation."[3]

The most influential writings were *The Craftsman,* Bolingbroke's journal, and *Cato's Letters. The Craftsman* "was drawn on repeatedly, paraphrased, quoted, cribbed,—cited in some of the least likely circumstances as 'the most masterly performance that ever was wrote upon the British constitution.' "[4] No less influential was *Cato's Letters,* which was reprinted continually throughout the colonies. Richard Hofstadter asserts that it was "a source so revered in eighteenth-century America that . . . it outstripped Locke in frequency of reference and perhaps in influence as well."[5] According to many colonists, corruption had become so pervasive in Britain that it threatened the British Constitution. The colonists took the jeremiads of Bolingbroke and the radical Whigs to heart. The arbitrary power fostered by corruption, it was commonly thought, would ultimately encroach upon their own liberty.

Why was the patriotism of Bolingbroke and the radical Whigs, with their talk of plots, cabals, and designs, more popular in the colonies than in Britain? Perhaps the answer lies in the difference in the political landscapes of the home country and the colonies, which made the political situation in the colonies inherently unstable. In the colonies, for example, the notion of deference implied in the organization of society into the three estates of King, Lords, and Commons was not generally accepted. In a sense, neither governors nor governed knew where they stood politically. Such confusion inevitably led to fears on both sides: The governors suspected many colonists of trying to subvert their authority, and the colonists suspected many governors of trying to subvert their liberty. Thomas Hutchinson, the governor of Massachusetts, had little doubt that colonial unrest was caused by a secret, power-hungry cabal that professed loyalty to Britain while it endeavored to destroy the bonds of authority between Britain and the colonies. And many colonists, in their turn, regarded Hutchinson as a man tainted with the corruption endemic in Britain, a man engaged in a secret design to sacrifice the general welfare to advance his own private interests.[6]

The colonists not only closely watched the actions of the governors but also kept abreast of events in Britain, which they considered portents of things to come in the colonies. During the years immediately before the Revolution, the colonists were especially aroused by the Wilkes affair. His being denied the seat in Parliament to which he had been elected was more evidence that British "influence"—that is, the crown's power by dint of its corruption—was destroying liberty. Wilkes's exclusion confirmed their suspicions that the ministry in power was engaged in a palpable design to subvert the British Constitution. Unless drastic measures were taken, they thought, the arbitrary power of the crown would continue to make itself felt in the colonies. As one colonist put it, "The fate of Wilkes and America must stand or fall together."[7]

The colonists ascribed great significance to the Wilkes affair. They understood it, as they understood many events of the decade before the Revolution, as the sign of an alarming crisis. The patriotic cast of mind, rich in suspicion, read into every action a significance that often was not there. Even Burke, who objected to Britain's American policy, states in "Speech on Conciliation with the Colonies" that the colonists tended to blow things out of proportion. "In other colonies, the people, more simple, and of a less mercurial cast, judge of an ill principle in government by an actual grievance; here [in the American colonies] they anticipate the evil, and judge of the pressure of the grievance by the badness of the principle."[8] Colonial patriots were inclined to invoke principles whenever they could—inclined, that is, to conduct themselves as if they belonged to parties from principle, to use Hume's terms, rather than parties from interest. "Disputes of the crassest, least principled character," Bailyn writes, "skidded off their original tracks onto elevating planes of disputation and ended deadlocked in the realm of principle."[9]

The patriotic rhetoric that infected colonial politics made it inevitable that differences over matters of policy were exacerbated, breeding a distrust so great that the only recourse possible for most colonists was a complete break with Britain. Yet the change in regime brought about by the revolutionary war did not cause the patriotic cast of mind to disappear. The citizens of the Republic no longer had to worry about the influence of the crown but they retained "habits of soreness, jealousy, and distrust," as Burke would say.[10] Whatever unity of purpose that had existed during the revolutionary war soon began to unravel: The people distrusted the politicians and the country was filled with factions that distrusted one another. The prognosis was not good, for the colonial experience made it unlikely that the country would hold together. "The history of politics in eighteenth-century America," Bailyn observes, "is the history of a factionalism born of a political system . . . lacking in what any objective observer would consider a minimal degree of functional integration."[11] Joseph Priestly, an English radical Whig and American sympathizer, stated that "it was taken for granted that the moment America had thrown off the yoke of Great Britain, the different states would go to war among themselves."[12]

Burke, in "A Letter to the Sheriffs of Bristol," claims that all polities need to nurture an "unsuspecting confidence" on the part of the governed towards those who govern them. Such a confidence "removes all difficulties, and reconciles all the contradictions which occur in the complexity of all ancient puzzled political establishments." And he adds: "Happy are the rulers which have the secret of preserving it!"[13] The question uppermost in the minds of some American statesmen, however, was not how to preserve an unsuspecting confidence but how to build any trust at all. Many Americans had a patriotic cast of mind that made them constantly alert for conspiracies against the public interest, and many others had a Puritan suspicion of all power. When Samuel Adams declared that "ambition and lust for power above the law are . . . predominant passions in the breasts of most men,"[14] he was uttering a commonplace of eighteenth-century American thought.

In England, patriots were not so suspicious of power. Tory patriots like Bolingbroke believed that one class—the landed aristocracy—could safely be entrusted with power. And even the radical Whigs were less inclined than many Americans to attack power in itself rather than the power of the moneyed interest, which controlled (so they argued) Walpole's ministry. But many Americans did not regard power as something to keep from bad or weak men; it was something that changed good men to bad—"converts a good man in private life to a tyrant in office." Power is addictive; once someone tastes it, he wants to increase the dose. "Ambition and thirst for sway are so deeply implanted in the human mind," asserted an editorial in the *New York Mercury* in 1755, "that one degree of elevation serves only as a step by which to ascend the next. . . ." And since "lust of domination" is rooted in human nature, it is stupid to "entrust any set of people with more power than necessity requires."[15]

What, though, did necessity require? Most Americans were not out-and-out anarchists; they knew some forms of delegated authority were required, but they hoped to check the aggrandizing nature of power by keeping government as local as possible. "What do frequent Elections avail," Samuel Adams said, "without that Spirit of Jealousy and Strict Inquiry which alone can render such Elections any Security to the People?"[16] Although many Americans agreed with Adams that the citizenry should keep a close eye on those entrusted with power, the preference for local government was to some degree the result of distinctive electoral customs. In Britain any constituency could be represented by any candidate, regardless of residence, whereas in the colonies residency requirements were usually the rule. The practice encouraged representatives to think of themselves as speakers predominantly for the interests of their constituencies, especially because many representatives were held strictly accountable to local electorates by means of binding instructions.

There were other reasons that many Americans thought it was important to keep governments as local as possible. It was a commonplace of political thought—a commonplace reiterated by Montesquieu, a writer much read by Americans—that republican governments were appropriate for small territories only. An extended republic, Patrick Henry argued, was "a work too great for human wisdom." An anonymous southern writer echoed the sentiment: "It is impossible for the same code of laws to suit Georgia and Massachusetts."[17] Americans were very much aware of the cultural diversity among the peoples of the thirteen states, and of their different economic interests. Although most Americans were, as Herbert Storing describes them, "irrevocably committed to a commercial order,"[18] many also thought it important to foster a citizenry imbued with civic virtue, and they doubted civic virtue could flourish in an extended republic. In a national government very few people would participate in politics, making it difficult to cultivate a sense of what the public interest may require. A national government was unworkable, argued the Anti-Federalists. (This was the name given to those who opposed the ratification of the Constitution.) As one Anti-Federalist wrote: "In a republic, the manners, sentiments, and interests of the people should be similar. If this be not the case, there will be a constant clashing of opinions; and the representatives of one part will be continually striving against those of the other. This will retard the operation of government, and prevent such conclusions as will promote the public good."[19] Many Americans, then, thought that the public interest was best served by having strong state governments and a weak national government.

A weak national government is what they got. The Articles of Confederation, submitted to the states for ratification in November 1777 and ratified finally by Maryland (the last holdout) in March 1781, provided the basis for a government that was merely an agency for cooperation among the state governments. Each state retained its sovereignty and independence. There was no provision for an executive or a permanent judiciary. Congress was granted no control over commerce among the states and with foreign countries. Furthermore, the Articles failed to give Congress its own taxing powers. The Articles of Confederation may have provided for the form of government best suited to the temper of the times, but its center was so weak that the conduct of foreign affairs was made well-nigh impossible and the defense of the nation exceedingly difficult. The center could not hold because, in fact, there was no center. Some Americans, including Alexander Hamilton and James Madison, were not sanguine about the future of the Republic unless drastic changes were made. Without more power vested in a national government, the new nation would be at the mercy of foreign nations.

Madison himself had to some extent a patriotic cast of mind. He had praised civic virtue as a force that would prevent any tyrannical power from "putting the yoke on us." By the mid-1780s, however, he had come to think that liberty was less in danger of being undermined by a strong central government than by the federal system then in place, for many states had constitutions that provided no checks against the despotism of a legislative majority. "Wherever the real power in a Government lies," he told Jefferson, "there is the danger of oppression. In our Governments the real power lies in the majority of the Community, and the invasion of private rights is chiefly to be apprehended, not from acts of Government contrary to the sense of its constituents, but from acts in which the Government is the mere instrument of the major number of the constituents."[20]

According to Madison, many Americans had escaped the yoke of Britain only to find themselves under the yoke of state legislatures that flouted the rights of minorities. It seemed that American political life in the 1780s had called "into question the fundamental principle of republican Government, that the majority who rule in such governments are the safest Guardians both of public Good and private rights." There was little to fear from the traditional abuse of power by the few over the many. "It is much more to be dreaded that the few will be unnecessarily sacrificed to the many."[21]

Madison worried about democratic disorder as well as democratic despotism. He began in 1785 to warn that unless the Union were strengthened there would be a system of jealous sovereign states that would result in "an appeal to the sword in every petty squabble." Internal weaknesses would make the disunited states "the sport of foreign politics, threaten the very existence of liberty, and blast the glory of the Revolution." The weaknesses of the Federation, he feared, would cause the new Republic to "tumble to the ground."[22]

At the time of the Constitutional Convention, many Americans thought the new Republic was in serious difficulties and that it might even collapse. George Washington, writing to Madison after Shay's Rebellion in 1786, reflected gloomily that "in so short a space we should have made such large strides towards fulfilling the predictions of our transatlantic foe. 'Leave them to themselves and their government will soon dissolve'. . . . What stronger evidence can be given of the want of energy in our government than these disorders?"[23] According to Herbert Storing, "Few Anti-Federalists would in fact have objected to the designation of 1787 as the 'critical period,' and many used that or synonymous phrases."[24]

The problem of democratic despotism as well as the general difficulties of governance under the Articles of Confederation led Hamilton and Madison to question some of the basic tenets of the patriotic tradition. Civil discord in the states, they came to realize, could not be explained by corruption. Corruption in its technical sense, of course, did not apply, because under the Articles of Confederation there was no equivalent of the crown to influence the thirteen legislatures. And even if there was corruption in its general sense, it did not explain why the legislatures were filled with what Adam Smith called "rancorous and violent factions."[25] To believe that calls for civic virtue and patriotism would prove effective remedies for the disorders of the Confederation made little sense to Madison and Hamilton. Hamilton said in 1782 that "we may preach, till we are tired of the theme, the necessity of disinterestedness in republics, without making a single proselyte. The virtuous declaimer will neither persuade himself nor any other person to be content with a double mess of porridge, instead of a reasonable stipend for his services."[26] The patriotic tradition, which had fired the colonists in their struggle with Britain, was of little help in resolving the problems of the postwar era. The nation was suffering not from corruption, Madison and Hamilton decided, but from the diseases traditionally associated with republican government, a form of government that most political thinkers believed was inherently unstable because it tended to spawn violent factions.

Some other Americans continued to view the political situation in patriotic terms, but, like all their countrymen, they were aware of the problems. Patrick Henry, for example, feared "that our Body politic was dangerously sick."[27] There were calls for a greater dose of patriotism, denunciations of private interest, and appeals for a renewal of civic virtue. Samuel Adams complained that in Boston "a Spirit of Avarice" was becoming predominant and, if allowed to prevail, would destroy the Republic. "Neither the wisest constitution nor the wisest laws will secure the liberty and happiness of a people whose manners are universally corrupt."[28] Adams had hoped that out of the ordeal of the revolution there would emerge a republic whose citizenry would profess the same virtues as had the ancient Spartans: simplicity, frugality, temperance, and, above all, devotion to the public interest. If other patriots were less inclined to invoke Sparta, they too complained of "the many Mandevilles, who laugh at virtue," as Richard Henry Lee said. Another patriot argued that "the bane of patriotism" was commerce.[29] Many Americans, it was clear, still carried their prewar baggage of patriotic suspicions with them—suspicion of commerce in general but suspicion especially of false patriots, men who would betray the public interest to advance their private interests.

Despite his increasing dissatisfaction with the patriotic tradition, Madison still regarded himself as a republican, someone who believed that the American government derives its legitimacy from the people. Therefore he sought, as he says in *Federalist* 10, a "republican remedy for the diseases most incident to republican government."[30] To find this remedy, Madison in the winter of 1785–86 immersed himself in the two hundred volumes of history and political theory that he had instructed Jefferson to send him from Paris. Having intensively studied what he called "the science of federal government," Madison was probably the best-prepared delegate to the Constitutional Convention, which he and Alexander Hamilton were instrumental in organizing, as Madison said, to render the federal constitution "adequate to the exigencies of the Union."[31]

Madison's awareness of the present discontents as well as his knowledge of how republican confederacies had fared in the past convinced him, he wrote to Edmund Randolph, that a "systematic change" in the nature of the American government was necessary. If the Republic was to survive, it needed to undergo reform that would "strike . . . deeply at the old Confederation."[32] What Madison had in mind, as he made clear at the Constitutional Convention, was his Virginia Plan, a scheme for the formation of a strong national government. It struck too deeply for most members of the convention, and the Constitution that was adopted was more respectful, as Marvin Meyers remarks, toward states' rights than Madison's original proposals and arguments had been. Indeed, Madison himself had acknowledged that his plan might be too radical, for he said to Randolph that the delegates "scarcely admit of the expedient."[33]

As many commentators have pointed out, Madison's defense of a strong central government relies on the British scientists of politics, especially David Hume. Like Hume, Madison thought the rise of commerce made it less likely that violent factions—what Hume calls parties from principle— would develop. In *Federalist* 10 Madison concedes that violent factions could arise because people have a "zeal for different opinions," but in "civilized"—that is, predominantly commercial—societies factions are usually based on different economic interests. "A landed interest, a manufacturing interest, a mercantile interest, a moneyed interest, with many lesser interests grow up of necessity in civilized nations, and divide them into different classes, actuated by different sentiments and views." Madison makes it clear that such factions are less likely to be zealous—less likely to "vex and oppress each other"—than are factions based on different views of religion and government. In short, these factions can be *regulated.* "The regulation of these various and interfering interests forms the principal task of modern legislation and involves the spirit of party and faction in the necessary and ordinary operations of government."[34] The key word is "modern": Such interests exist only in modern—that is, predominantly commercial—polities. The expansion of commerce not only makes a patriotic politics anachronistic and impracticable but also helps to reduce the likelihood of violent factional discord.

What was the alternative? American politicians, Madison says in *Federalist* 10, could follow Hobbes's or Bolingbroke's prescriptions for dealing with factions; they could extinguish the liberty that is essential to the existence of factions or they could exhort the people to have "the same opinions, the same passions, and the same interests."[35] The former course of action clearly was unacceptable; the latter was impracticable, indeed utopian. In modern polities factions inevitably exist, but it was important to persuade each faction not to make believe that it was a party from principle, that it alone carried the flag of the public interest; it was important to convince each faction that it basically stood for economic concerns and therefore had to let itself be "regulated" by national legislators.

Madison was also influenced by another idea of Hume's. In "Idea of a Perfect Commonwealth," Hume says that "though it is more difficult to form a republican government in an extensive country than in a city, there is more facility, when once it is formed, of preserving it steady and uniform without tumult and faction."[36] Its very size makes it difficult for parts to combine against the public interest. Contradicting Montesquieu and Patrick Henry, Madison makes much the same point. In an extended republic, he says in *Federalist* 51, "the society will itself be broken into so many parts, interests, and classes of citizens that the rights of individuals, or of the minority, will be in little danger from interested combinations of the majority." An extended republic, therefore, solves the problem of democratic despotism—a majority faction tyrannizing a minority—because each faction is forced to seek some common ground with other factions. "In the extended republic . . . a coalition of the majority of the whole society could seldom take place on any other principles than those of justice and the general good."[37] Madison was hopeful that in an extended republic composed in the main of parties from interest rather than parties from principle, the process of building coalitions to get legislation enacted would tend to discipline and moderate factions, tend to make them less inclined to resort to the language of accusation.

Insofar as the Constitution adopted in Philadelphia made it clear that sovereignty resided in the people, Madison truly thought it was a republican remedy for the diseases most incident to republican government. But most patriots did not agree. Indeed, many Americans doubted that a republic could flourish in an extended territory. And some thought, as Patrick Henry did, that the Constitution was a plot to undermine the liberty of the people. In a speech criticizing the work of the Constitutional Convention, Henry said that "the tyranny of Philadelphia may be like the tyranny of George III." Samuel Adams, although he eventually voted for ratification, had similar thoughts: "I confess, as I enter the Building"—enter, that is, the new governmental structure outlined in the Constitution—"I stumble at the threshhold. I meet with a National Government, instead of a Federal Union of Sovereign States."[38]

Madison, of course, was aware of the problem of convincing doubters that the Constitution would not undermine the liberty of Americans. In *Federalist* 37, he acknowledges that "among the difficulties encountered by the convention, a very important one must have lain in combining the requisite stability and energy in government with the inviolable attention due to liberty and to the republican form."[39] He, in fact, believed the convention had adopted a Constitution that lacked sufficient energy, but most Americans were probably on Henry's and Adams's side; they thought the Constitution would weaken their liberty mainly because it set up a national government that would meet in a distant capital so that legislators would not be closely watched by the people. As Samuel Adams said: "There is a Degree of Watchfulness over all Men possessed of Power or Influence upon which the Liberties of Mankind much depend. It is necessary to guard against the Infirmities of the best as well as the Wickedness of the worst of Men. . . . Jealousy is the best Security of publick Liberty."[40] Madison thought such political jealousy could prevent the new republic from having energy sufficient to sustain itself. But how could he convince patriotic doubters such as Adams that the government envisioned in the Constitution would not destroy the liberty of Americans? He did not expect to be able to persuade patriots to have an unsuspecting confidence, as Burke would put it, in the new national government, but he did hope to make them see that it was the lesser evil—that unless the Constitution was ratified the states would remain in dire straits. Such was the task he set himself— together with Hamilton and Jay—when he wrote, under the pen name of Publius, *The Federalist*.

Publius's Persuasion

Writing to Jefferson in 1825, Madison said that *The Federalist* should be regarded "as the most authentic exposition of the text of the federal Constitution."[41] He may have been right, but *The Federalist* was written not primarily to explain the Constitution but to persuade delegates in the key states of New York and Virginia to vote for ratification. By speaking of Publius rather than of Madison, Hamilton, and Jay, we are reminded that *The Federalist* was first and foremost an electioneering pamphlet, one in which the collaborators tailored their arguments and chose their words to fit the task at hand: changing the minds of some Anti-Federalists. The men who wrote *The Federalist* were wearing masks; they were acting as public men intent on persuasion, not as private men discoursing on the nature of government under the new Constitution. The author is Publius, not Madison, Hamilton, and Jay.

The Federalist does not have a tight structure nor a uniform style, for it was composed hastily, with assignments changing because of Jay's illness and Madison's need to return to Virginia to qualify as a candidate for the ratifying convention. Although there is no question that particular essays have the stamp of Madison's, Hamilton's, or Jay's (Jay wrote only five essays) notions of governance, those by Madison cannot be said to be the thought of Madison in the same sense that essays by Hume are the thought of Hume. Madison's contributions are a lucid exposition of ideas he had worked out in previous letters and essays, but the ideas have been bent, as it were, by the pressures of the moment. They are, above all, politic ideas, prudential ideas calculated not to arouse the ire or inflame the suspicions of Anti-Federalists. They are the thoughts of Madison with his mask on, and they are less than candid.

Writing as Publius, Madison did not divulge his private reservations about the Constitution. Both he and Hamilton had wanted something different—a constitution with more powers vested in a central government. Hamilton's arguments at the New York ratifying convention, in fact, were regarded with incredulity by some contemporaries, one of whom said: "You would be surprised did you not know the Man, what an *amazing Republican* Hamilton wishes to make himself be considered."[42] Hamilton and Madison, moreover, had little in common. Hamilton, as characterized by Douglass Adair, was a man whose "personal tastes, amusements, habits of life, and political ideas were poles apart" from Madison's.[43] But both put on the mask of Publius because they agreed that ratifying the Constitution was a wiser course of action than continuing with the Articles of Confederation.

The odds were against Madison and Hamilton. The majority of Americans probably were Anti-Federalists. In New York the Federalists were outnumbered three to one; in Virginia, by slightly more than a majority.[44] Yet the Federalists triumphed in both states. The victory in Virginia may have been influenced by *The Federalist,* but it is doubtful that it played an important part in New York. By the time the New York convention began on 17 June 1788, eight states had already ratified the Constitution and both Virginia and New Hampshire were expected to do so a week later. Because the Constitution became law while New York was deliberating about it, the debate centered less on its merits than on whether or not New York should join the Union. Yet nine months earlier, when Madison, Hamilton, and Jay had decided to collaborate under the name of Publius, they had no way of knowing what the fate of the Constitution would be. Although they knew that George Washington's support of the Constitution would be more persuasive than anything they might write, they thought that a collection of essays that explained the Federalist point of view might be useful in itself and might also help other Federalists in their debates with Anti-Federalists.

As men who became Publius, the authors of *The Federalist* knew that to be successful at persuasion they had to pay careful attention to rhetoric. In modern times, the term "rhetoric" has often had a pejorative connotation. When a speech is dismissed as "mere rhetoric," it means that it evades the question at hand. Rhetoric, however, was not so regarded in the eighteenth century. Gordon S. Wood tells us that "rhetoric lay at the heart of an eighteenth century liberal education and was regarded as a necessary mark of a gentleman and an indispensable skill for a statesman, especially for a statesman in a republic."[45] In his *Autobiography,* Franklin celebrates the art of rhetoric; and Thomas Jefferson listed rhetoric as a prominent part of the curriculum he planned for the University of Virginia.

One of the texts that Jefferson no doubt would have wanted to include in his curriculum is Aristotle's *Rhetoric.* According to Aristotle, there are three kinds of rhetoric: deliberative or political rhetoric; forensic or judicial rhetoric; and epideictic or declamatory rhetoric. Deliberative or political rhetoric is the kind appropriate for speeches giving counsel or advice, specifically advising a legislative body which course of action is more advantageous and expedient. Whether or not he knew his Aristotle, Publius realized that the question of ratification called for deliberative rhetoric. He says in the opening sentence of *Federalist* 1: "After an unequivocal experience of the inefficiency of the subsisting federal government, you are called upon to deliberate on a new Constitution for the United States of America."[46] Publius is trying to convince the delegates to the state ratifying conventions that ratifying the Constitution is the wiser course of action.

In asking his audience to recognize that the occasion called for deliberation, Publius was well aware that its members were steeped in the language of the patriotic tradition, essentially a language that conformed to Aristotle's notion of declamatory rhetoric—a language more suited to praise and blame than to counsel and advice. Declamatory rhetoric may have been appropriate during the revolutionary war when, as Publius says in *Federalist* 49, the external danger gave people "an enthusiastic confidence . . . in their patriotic leaders, which stifled the ordinary diversity of opinions on great national questions. . . ."[47] What was needed then was not a rhetoric suitable for decision making, for the decision had already been made, but a rhetoric that would incite greater effort in the struggle. But such rhetoric was not appropriate to an occasion when men had to decide, as Publius says in *Federalist* 62, which was the lesser evil. The declamatory rhetoric of the patriotic tradition inevitably would turn disagreement over which course of action to take into occasions for praise and blame. As a result, both sides would find themselves locked into what each regarded as the only honorable position, and persuasion would not take place. Publius knew that it would have been morally wrong as well as tactically foolish to call the Anti-Federalist position dishonorable.

Nevertheless, Publius could not altogether avoid using declamatory rhetoric. He faced a dilemma: if he said that patriotic language should be dispensed with, he might be accused of going against the American grain; yet, if he used such language, it would lead him to attack those who disagreed with him as false patriots, as men swayed by private interest. The latter tactic, Publius knew, would be divisive and would gain few adherents to the Federalist position, yet the former tactic was perhaps the greater risk, because the Federalists were suspected of being counterrevolutionaries, men advocating a political system that departed dramatically from republican notions of governance.

Publius hoped to resolve the dilemma by trying to escape from it. He makes use of declamatory rhetoric to establish his credentials as a patriot, but a new kind of patriot—one who thinks the realities of the postwar era require a different polity and a different political language. Publius proposes a significant change from patriotic notions of politics but at the same time he argues that what he proposes is consonant with the principles and spirit of the Revolution—is, indeed, a fulfillment of them. This tricky rhetorical device leads him to bend the truth somewhat. The Constitution, he continually says, is "strictly Republican," yet in many ways it was at variance with traditional notions of republican government; the Constitution, he says, accords with the ideas of Montesquieu, yet in many ways it departed from Montesquieu's notions of governance; and the Constitution, he says, received unanimous approval at the Constitutional Convention, but he neglects to add that only a technicality of parliamentary procedure enabled the negative votes of Elbridge Gerry, Edmund Randolph, and George Mason to go unrecorded.

To establish his credentials as a patriot, Publius also resorts at times to a potentially dangerous ploy: He attacks the Anti-Federalist position as unpatriotic. In *Federalist* 14, for example, he claims that the Anti-Federalists are "advocates for disunion" who speak in an "unnatural voice." The ordeal of the Revolution, he says, created a patriotic "family" that will be destroyed unless the Constitution is ratified. Moreover, in *Federalist* 37, Publius claims that the unanimity of the Constitutional Convention is a sign that God is on the side of the Federalists. "It is impossible for the man of pious reflection not to perceive in it a finger of that Almighty hand which has been so frequently and signally extended to our relief in the critical stages of the revolution." Finally, he argues in *Federalist* 62 that the Anti-Federalists are contributing to the decline of patriotism because they support a government that does not command the respect of the people. A diminution of attachment and reverence inevitably "steals into the hearts of the people towards a political system which betrays so many marks of infirmity, and disappoints so many of their flattering hopes."[48]

Publius chose to end *The Federalist* on a ringingly patriotic note. Warning against calling for another constitutional convention in the hope of arriving at a better constitution, Publius declares in *Federalist* 85: "I dread the more the consequences of new attempts because I KNOW that POW-

ERFUL INDIVIDUALS, in this and in other States, are enemies to a general national government in every possible shape." The language—even the typography—recalls "The Watchman" and other patriotic tracts that hinted darkly of conspiracies. In an earlier passage in the essay, Publius indignantly denies that the Federalists were engaged in a "conspiracy against the liberties of the people."[49] In this final patriotic flourish, which is the last sentence of the last essay, Publius implies that charges of conspiracy should be leveled against those Anti-Federalists who refuse even to deliberate about the Constitution. For reasons known only to themselves—sinister reasons, Publius implies—their minds have been made up beforehand. Publius probably realized that this rhetorical trick was shabby but hoped that some Anti-Federalists might swallow the insinuations and turn Federalist.

Few Anti-Federalists, I imagine, were convinced by such rhetoric. Insofar as the Anti-Federalists regarded an extended republic as a contradiction in terms, they probably thought that ratifying the Constitution would ultimately shatter the bonds of the American family and hasten the decline of patriotism. And they must have doubted that God could be on the side of a government that resembled the one they had just overthrown, a government that would be tainted with the corruption that went hand in hand with despotic authority. The creation of a strong central government, the Anti-Federalists maintained, would abet corruption and undermine liberty. Publius's patriotic claims could only encourage patriotic counterclaims, and his questioning of the Anti-Federalists' motives could only lead them to question his motives. Charges would lead to countercharges, with the result that the relative merits of the Constitution would not be weighed.

Thus, Publius obviously uses patriotic rhetoric, but mainly to wean the Anti-Federalists from it—to impress upon them that the question before them requires deliberation, not declamation. In *Federalist* 1 he makes it clear that he will avoid questioning the motives of those who disagree with him. "It would be disingenuous to resolve indiscriminately the opposition of any set of men . . . into interested or ambitious views." It is disingenuous, Publius suggests, because one can never isolate another's motives; one cannot even isolate one's own. Like La Rochefoucauld, Publius thinks that it is impossible to disentangle motives: Those who oppose us may be motivated in part by less than noble reasons, but our own views may be less than noble as well. Even if we could fathom someone's motives, such knowledge would get us nowhere because there is no clear connection between honorable motives and sound policies. Many wise and good men, Publius says, are often "on the wrong as well as on the right side of questions of the first magnitude to society." He adds that "ambition, avarice, personal animosity, party opposition, and many other motives not more laudable than these, are apt to operate as well upon those who support as those who oppose the right side of a question."[50]

According to Publius, motive-hunting is not only irrelevant to the process of deliberation but also harmful to it. Motive-hunting increases the distrust that exists among men who hold different views on an issue, because inevitably each thinks that he is pure at heart and the others are not. The result is "a torrent of angry and malignant passions," a climate of intolerance that makes it difficult for deliberation to take place. Publius realized that no matter what he said, some Anti-Federalists would prefer to look through his arguments to see if they could discover his motives, but he hoped that at least some Anti-Federalists would be persuaded to understand that it was in the public interest to examine the arguments in their own right, divorced from the men who propounded them. "My motives," he says, "must remain in the depository of my own breast. My arguments will be open to all and may be judged of by all."[51] To stress the importance of refraining from motive-hunting, Publius pointedly refused to speak of his motives.

For deliberation to take place, then, each side should refrain from speculating about the motives of the other and instead focus on the arguments advanced. Publius's deliberative strategy is simple. He first asserts that the Republic is suffering from a crisis because it is afflicted by the diseases "most incident to republican government." He then offers a remedy that he says has been made possible by the greatly improved science of politics: an extended republic composed of numerous factions, predominantly parties from interest—to use Hume's phrase—rather than parties from principle. The majority of the essays are taken up with persuading the Anti-Federalists that this remedy "is the best which our political situation, habits, and opinions will admit, and superior to any the revolution has produced"—superior, that is, to all the remedies the patriots have advanced. The remedy, he grants, is not perfect, because "the results of the deliberations of all collective bodies," Publius says in *Federalist* 85, "must necessarily be a compound, as well of the errors and prejudices as of the good sense and wisdom of the individuals of whom they are composed. The compacts which are to embrace thirteen distinct States in a common bond of amity and union must as necessarily be a compromise of as many dissimilar interests and inclinations. How can perfection spring from such materials?" Those who prefer to continue with the Confederation in the hope of attaining perfection, Publius says in the last paragraph, are "hazarding anarchy, civil war, a perpetual alienation of the States from each other, and perhaps the military despotism of a victorious demagogue. . . ."[52] The best, Publius implies, is the enemy of the good.

It was one thing to convince Anti-Federalists that republican confedera-

cies were prone to certain diseases, for Publius could support his argument
with evidence from history, but it was another to convince Anti-Federalists
that his remedy for the diseases was the best available. It had never been
tested. The kind of political system that Publius was proposing—an extended republic with a strong central government—had never existed. How
could the Anti-Federalists be certain that it would not result in the destruction of their liberty, especially because republican "Jealousy" could not
operate effectively when legislators in a national capital were so removed
from the watchmen?

The Anti-Federalists, according to one historian, were men of little faith
in an extended republic with a strong central government, but their fears
were far from groundless. As Edmund S. Morgan points out, they thought
this new leviathan would destroy the state governments and ultimately their
liberty. And they thought that "a national government by its very nature,
by virtue of the size of the area it governed, would be incapable of recogniz-
ing, or responding to, the needs of the people. . . ."[53] Publius realized that
simply by advocating a stronger national government, he would be accused
of subverting liberty. "An enlightened zeal for the energy and efficiency of
government," he says in *Federalist* 1, "will be stigmatized as the offspring
of a temper fond of despotic power and hostile to the principles of liberty."[54]

Publius tries to overcome this difficulty by arguing that his character is
beside the point. Even if he is "fond of despotic power and hostile to the
principles of liberty," the political system provided for in the Constitution
would prevent him or any potential despots from succeeding in their designs. In such an extended republic, ambition would be made to counteract
ambition, and "the defect of better motives"—the lack, that is, of civic
virtue on the part of many Americans—would not prove dangerous to
liberty because "opposite and rival interests" would make it impossible for
any one faction to become an "overbearing majority." In a small republic,
a majority faction can ride roughshod over the rights of minorities, but in
a large republic no one faction will be able to "invade the rights of other
citizens." In *Federalist* 10 Publius says that the advantage of a large republic
consists "in the greater security afforded by a greater variety of parties,
against the event of any one party being able to outnumber and oppress the
rest."[55]

In the attempt to overcome distrust, Publius is also making a more
general point about the language of politics. Advising the delegates to vote
for ratification, he is also advising them to adopt a new kind of political
language, one in which the word "interest" is central. Publius argues that
in an extended republic, where most factions will be parties from interest
rather than parties from principle, politics will be taken up with seeking
accommodations among interests. The new system is trustworthy, Publius

argues, because private interest—not disinterest—is the engine that makes it run. Whereas patriots called for disinterested watchmen to guard jealously their liberty, Publius hopes that under the new political system "the private interest of every individual may be a sentinel over the public rights."[56] There will be no true patriots or false patriots; there will only be men with different "sentiments and views" that arise out of their different interests—arise, that is, out of their economic concerns.

But the problem of distrust was not so easily overcome. Deliberation, according to Aristotle, is a question of probabilities, the likelihood that if x is chosen y will occur. If the delegates so distrusted Publius they would also distrust his assessment of the probabilities: in an extended republic a majority faction is an unlikely phenomenon. In any case, some Anti-Federalists thought all discussions of how the new political system would work should be regarded warily because they led one's mind away from the Constitution itself. As one Anti-Federalist said: "The System ought to speak for itself; and not need Explanations." Most Anti-Federalists were inclined to dismiss Publius's arguments—and, indeed, the arguments of all Federalists—as too clever. One Anti-Federalist at the Massachusetts ratifying convention forecast: "These lawyers and men of learning and moneyed men that talk so finely and gloss over matters so smoothly . . . will swallow all of us little folks like the great Leviathan. . . ." Finally, few Anti-Federalists, I imagine, actually read what Publius had to say, and they probably were content to dismiss whatever the Federalists said as part of a plot. Asked why he had refused to accept a place on the Virginia delegation to the Constitutional Convention, Patrick Henry declared only that he had "smelt a rat."[57]

It would be wrong, however, to argue that only Anti-Federalists "smelt a rat." Like the Anti-Federalists, the Federalists often resorted to the language of the patriotic tradition, speaking of plots, conspiracies, designs. Madison, himself, in an effort to discredit his most formidable opponent and win over the wavering Edmund Randolph, said to Randolph that Patrick Henry (the leader of the Anti-Federalists in Virginia) wanted to set up a Southern confederacy, and that Henry preferred a different Constitution in order "to render it subservient to his real designs."[58] Yet, most historians think that the Anti-Federalists were more guilty than the Federalists of using the language of praise and blame. According to Robert A. Rutland, "Antifederalists worked overtime at undermining Federalist reputations. They poured torrents of abuse on the Federalists, insinuating that theirs was the party of aristocratic, would-be royalists."[59] The difference between the rhetoric of the Federalists and the rhetoric of the Anti-Federalists may have been a key factor in the debate that took place at the Virginia ratifying

convention, where the Constitution was approved by the narrow margin of
10 out of 168 votes.

The principal debaters were Patrick Henry and James Madison. Henry
was clearly a power to be reckoned with; he could cast a spell not by the
logic of his argument, which even his defenders admitted was loose, but by
his oratory. As one Federalist said, "There is no accounting for the effects
which Mr. Henry's address and Rhetoric may have upon them [the dele-
gates] afterwards."[60] Far more widely known than Madison, Henry had a
large personal following in Virginia but failed in his effort to defeat ratification. For whatever reasons, ten delegates disregarded the express wishes of
their constituents and voted for ratification. Perhaps they were persuaded
by George Washington's support. Perhaps they also were persuaded by *The
Federalist* itself, for copies of the collected edition had been rushed to
Richmond at Hamilton's direction. Perhaps Patrick Henry simply defeated
himself, his declamations lacking in substance, filled with inflated charges.
Henry waxed so indignant about the potentially despotic authority of the
president that one reporter, tongue-in-cheek, wrote: "Here Mr. Henry
strongly and pathetically expatiated on the probability of the President's
enslaving America, and the horrid consequences that must result."[61]

Although the odds had been against them, the Federalists triumphed in
Virginia, partly because they were less inclined to use the rhetoric of the
patriotic tradition, a rhetoric that an increasing number of Americans
regarded as outmoded in a modern polity composed of "various and interfering interests." A revolutionary war pamphleteer from New York was
probably speaking for many Americans when in 1775 he said: "Tho' a truly
patriotic disposition would lead a man to reject every private advantage
inconsistent with the good of his country, yet no man is to be supposed so
disinterested, as not to include his own interest, in all his endeavors to
promote that of others."[62]

It would be wrong to assume that the Federalist victory meant the
demise of a patriotic politics. The main reason for the narrow win in
Virginia was the decision of Governor Edmund Randolph to throw his
support to the Federalists, and he did so because he thought that ratification
by eight states had made it impossible for Virginia not to ratify, impossible
because if it did not "the Union will be dissolved, the dogs of war will break
loose, and anarchy and discord will complete the ruin of this country."
Randolph acknowledged that he had reservations about the Constitution,
which he had refused to sign when he was a member of the Constitutional
Convention, but "its adoption is necessary to avoid the storm which is
hanging over America, and that no greater curse can befall her than the
dissolution of the political connection between the states."[63]

It is difficult, then, to assess the effect of the Federalist triumph on the patriotic approach to politics. Although some forty years later Tocqueville said that "the Americans enjoy explaining almost every act of their lives on the principle of self-interest properly understood,"[64] the language of political campaigning often has been infected with patriotic rhetoric. And the concerns of the Anti-Federalists often have made themselves felt in politics. Herbert Storing claims that "if . . . the foundation of the American polity was laid by the Federalists, the Anti-Federalist reservations echo through American history; and it is in the dialogue, not merely in the Federalist victory, that the country's principles are to be discovered."[65] Moreover, Madison and Hamilton, who adapted the principles of the science of politics for American use, never suggested that a patriotic approach to politics was completely wrong, never suggested that traditional republican theory, with its emphasis upon civic virtue, should be abandoned. Rather, they implied that it had to be modified. What they wanted was not an end to patriotism but a new kind of patriot.

Notes

1. Cited, Bernard Bailyn, *The Origins of American Politics* (New York: Alfred A. Knopf, 1968), pp. 140–41 (text and footnote).
2. Ibid.
3. Bernard Bailyn, *The Ideological Origins of the American Revolution* (Cambridge: Harvard University Press, 1972), p. 35.
4. Bailyn, *Origins of American Politics,* p. 55.
5. Richard Hofstadter, *The Idea of a Party System* (Berkeley: University of California Press, 1970), p. 14.
6. See Bernard Bailyn, *The Ordeal of Thomas Hutchinson* (Cambridge: Harvard University Press, 1974).
7. Cited, Bailyn, *Ideological Origins,* p. 112.
8. *Edmund Burke: Selected Works,* ed. W.J. Bate (New York: Random House, 1960), p. 127.
9. Bailyn, *Origins of American Politics,* p. 65.
10. Edmund Burke, "Letter to the Sheriffs of Bristol," in Bate, *Burke: Selected Works,* p. 217.
11. Bailyn, *Origins of American Politics,* p. 124.
12. Cited, Douglass Adair, *Fame and the Founding Fathers,* ed. Trevor Colbourn (New York: W. W. Norton, 1974), p. 117.
13. Bate, *Burke: Selected Works,* p. 215.
14. Cited, Bailyn, *Ideological Origins,* p. 60.
15. Ibid. See extended note, p. 61.
16. Cited, Gordon Wood, *The Creation of the American Republic, 1776–1787* (New York: W. W. Norton, 1972), p. 363.
17. Cited, Cecelia M. Kenyon, "Men of Little Faith: Anti-Federalists," in *Origins of American Political Thought,* ed. John P. Roche (New York: Harper & Row, 1967), p. 199; ibid., p. 200.
18. Herbert Storing, *What the Anti-Federalists Were For* (Chicago: University of Chicago Press, 1981), p. 46.

19. Cited, ibid., pp. 19–20.
20. Cited, Wood, *Creation of the American Republic*, pp. 102, 410.
21. Ibid., pp. 410, 413.
22. Cited, Adair, *Fame and the Founding Fathers*, p. 134.
23. Cited, Edmund S. Morgan, "A Sense of Power," *New Republic*, 21 February 1981, p. 29.
24. Storing, *What the Anti-Federalists Were For*, p. 26.
25. Cited, Donald Winch, *Adam Smith's Politics* (London: Cambridge University Press, 1978), p. 160.
26. *The Basic Ideas of Alexander Hamilton*, ed. Richard B. Morris (New York: Pocket Books, 1957), p. 69.
27. Cited, Wood, *Creation of the American Republic*, pp. 416–17.
28. Cited, Robert H. Horwitz, "John Locke and the Preservation of Liberty: A Perennial Problem of Civic Education," in *The Moral Foundations of the American Republic*, ed. Robert H. Horwitz (Charlottesville: University Press of Virginia, 1977), p. 131.
29. Cited, Wood, *Creation of the American Republic*, p. 420; ibid.
30. Clinton Rossiter, ed., *The Federalist Papers* (New York: New American Library, 1961), p. 84.
31. Cited, Wood, *Creation of the American Republic*, p. 472; cited, Marvin Meyers, ed., *The Mind of the Founder* (Indianapolis: Bobbs-Merrill, 1973), p. 69.
32. Cited, Wood, *Creation of the American Republic*, p. 473.
33. Meyers, *Mind of the Founder*, p. 94; Wood, *Creation of the American Republic*, p. 473.
34. Rossiter, *Federalist Papers*, p. 79.
35. Ibid., p. 78.
36. David Hume, "Idea of a Perfect Commonwealth," in *Hume's Political Essays*, ed. Charles W. Hendel (Indianapolis: Library of Liberal Arts, 1953), p. 157.
37. Rossiter, *Federalist Papers*, pp. 324–25.
38. Cited, Wood, *Creation of the American Republic*, p. 327; cited, ibid., p. 526.
39. Rossiter, *Federalist Papers*, p. 226.
40. Cited, Jackson Turner Main, *The Anti-Federalists: Critics of the Constitution* (Chapel Hill: University of North Carolina Press, 1961), p. 9.
41. Meyers, *Mind of the Founder*, p. 444.
42. Cited, Main, *Anti-Federalists*, p. 238.
43. Adair, *Fame and the Founding Fathers*, p. 60n.
44. See Robert A. Rutland, *The Ordeal of the Constitution* (Norman: University of Oklahoma Press, 1965).
45. Gordon S. Wood, "The Democratization of Mind in the American Revolution," in Horwitz, *Moral Foundations of the American Republic*, p. 110.
46. Rossiter, *Federalist Papers*, p. 33.
47. Ibid., p. 315.
48. Ibid., p. 103; p. 230; p. 382.
49. Ibid., p. 522; p. 527.
50. Ibid., p. 34.
51. Ibid., p. 35; p. 36.
52. Ibid., p. 523; p. 524; p. 527.
53. Edmund S. Morgan, "The Argument for the States," *New Republic*, 28 April 1982, p. 31.
54. Rossiter, *Federalist Papers*, p. 35.

55. Ibid., p. 322; p. 84.
56. Ibid., p. 322.
57. Cited, Main, *Anti-Federalists*, p. 154; cited, Wood, *Creation of the American Republic*, p. 487; cited, Rutland, *Ordeal of the Constitution*, p. 175.
58. See Rutland, *Ordeal of the Constitution*, p. 191.
59. Ibid., p. 41.
60. Ibid., p. 194.
61. Cited, Kenyon, "Men of Little Faith," p. 217n.
62. Cited, Pauline Maier, *The Old Revolutionaries: Political Lives in the Age of Samuel Adams* (New York: Alfred A. Knopf, 1980), p. 99n.
63. Cited, John J. Reardon, *Edmund Randolph: A Biography* (New York: Macmillan, 1974), pp. 147, 145.
64. Alexis de Tocqueville, *Democracy in America*, ed. J. P. Mayer (Garden City: Doubleday, 1969), p. 526.
65. Storing, *What the Anti-Federalists Were For*, p. 72.

3

A New Kind of Patriot

If *The Federalist* was instrumental in persuading some delegates to the Virginia ratifying convention to go against the wishes of their constituents, then it is perhaps the most important electioneering pamphlet in American history. After the Constitution was ratified, however, it sank into oblivion and was generally ignored by commentators. Rediscovered in the second decade of the twentieth century, it was interpreted in ways that would have astounded—or at least puzzled—Publius. The new readers of *The Federalist* realized the importance of interests to Publius's general argument, but either misunderstood why Publius spoke of interests in the first place or misunderstood what role Publius thought "various and interfering interests" would play in the governmental process.

The first writer to recognize the importance of *The Federalist* was the historian Charles Beard. Yet, in *An Economic Interpretation of the Constitution* Beard saw as his main task not to clarify what the proponents of the Constitution wanted but to unmask their motives. "Beard proclaimed that the proponents of the Constitution had maneuvered undemocratically to foist upon the nation a new federal system of government that represented the interests of the minority mercantile classes rather than those of the great mass of small farmers and debtors."[1] Beard raised Madison, the author of *Federalist* 10, into eminence again, but eminence of a dubious sort. According to Beard, the central idea of *Federalist* 10 is the following: "The theories of government which men entertain are emotional reactions to their property interests."[2]

Beard completely missed the point that for Madison there were opinions based on noneconomic concerns as well. There were, that is, parties from principle as well as parties from interest; and, for Madison, parties from principle are much more emotional—to use Beard's word—than parties from interest. Madison was not an economic determinist, but in a sense he wished that he could have been, because he thought that men were more amenable and accommodating when they were advancing their interests than when they were defending their principles. Beard misread Madison, but his argument makes no sense even on his own terms, for if Madison truly were defending the interests of a privileged class, he would not have said so. He would not have tried to persuade the Anti-Federalists—men supposedly holding economic interests opposed to his—to ratify a constitution that protected his interests, not theirs.

Its confusions notwithstanding, during the twenties and thirties Beard's reading of *The Federalist* became *the* reading for many historians. In the late forties, however, a different interpretation of *The Federalist* was offered by many political scientists. They cited *Federalists* 10 and 51 to show that one of the Founding Fathers had recognized the importance of interest groups in American politics. From the study of formal political institutions, they argued, one learned very little about the dynamics of the political process, very little about how political change really came about. One had to study interest groups. David Truman in *The Governmental Process,* a book that owes much to ideas about interest groups that were first broached by Arthur Bentley in *The Process of Government* (1908), cites *Federalist* 10 with approval. According to Truman, Madison was the Founding Father with the most wisdom and foresight; he knew how the American political system would work, he had discovered interest-group pluralism. "James Madison, whose brilliant analysis in the tenth essay in *The Federalist* we have often quoted," Truman says toward the end of the book, "relied primarily upon diversity of groups and difficulty of communication to protect the new government from the tyranny of a factious majority."[3]

Truman's reading of *Federalist* 10 is very different from Beard's, but neither Beard nor Truman shows any awareness of the distinction Madison makes between kinds of factions. And neither seems to realize that *Federalist* 10 is not an isolated text but part of a larger argument and must be interpreted within that context. Beard's reading, though, shows no understanding of Madison's thought, whereas Truman's is only a distortion of Madison's ideas, a distortion that is in some ways understandable if one looks at *Federalists* 10 and 51 in isolation.

Looking at the entire pamphlet, we can see why it is wrong to regard Madison as the founder of interest-group pluralism. Although he believed that "various and interfering interests" would play an important role, he never thought they would be at the center of the political process. Interests were the engine that would drive the American political system, but the machine needed someone to control it, someone to move it in the right direction. "The thrust of Madison's theory," Kenneth Morgan writes, "is that the stability of the political system depends chiefly upon the stability of the legislature."[4] Truman and other political scientists have underestimated the importance to Madison of national legislators, enlightened statesmen who, Madison says in *Federalist* 10, will "be able to adjust these clashing interests and render them all subservient to the public good."[5]

To see why *Federalists* 10 and 51 should not be considered the last word on Madison's theory of government, we have to see Madison with his mask on, see him as Publius—a man engaged in a difficult persuasive task. Convincing the Anti-Federalists that the current government was in dire straits was a relatively easy task for Publius; convincing them that the new government would not destroy their liberty was more difficult. Publius had to concede, to some degree, that the fears of the Anti-Federalists were reasonable. Therefore, he grants in *Federalist* 10 that "enlightened men will not always be at the helm," and, further, that in an extended republic it is possible that "men of factious tempers, of local prejudices, or of sinister designs, may, by intrigue, by corruption, or by other means, first obtain the suffrages, and then betray the interests of the people."[6] Speaking of "sinister designs," of "intrigue," and "corruption," Publius is using the standard language of the patriotic tradition, thereby showing the Anti-Federalists that he thinks their arguments have some merit.

Publius does not say, however, that in an extended republic enlightened men will *never* be at the helm but that the probability that national legislators would be enlightened men is greater than it would be in a small republic because candidates must appeal to a wide variety of voters and therefore are more likely to have "the most diffusive and established characters."[7] In other words, it is unlikely that someone who is unknown or idiosyncratic can get elected. But this point is not stressed in *Federalist* 10, for in this essay Publius builds his arguments upon the premises of the Anti-Federalists. He tries to convince them that even under what we might call "worst-case" conditions, even when enlightened statesmen are definitely not at the helm, liberty will be better protected than it is under the present system of government. The central point of *Federalist* 10 is that in an extended republic "various and interfering interests" will prevent any one interest from becoming an "overbearing majority."

The central point of *Federalist* 10 is not the central point of *The Federalist*. An argument based on the Anti-Federalists' fears of "sinister designs," Publius realizes, can be taken only so far. By building his case on the strong possibility that enlightened men may not be at the helm of government, Publius may be adding fuel to the fire of the Anti-Federalists' deep distrust of representative government. Therefore, Publius tries in the last third of *The Federalist* to convince the Anti-Federalists that their distrust is unreasonable because it exceeds all probability. A jealous regard for one's rights, Publius says in *Federalist* 51, is appropriate, but "an indiscriminate and unbounded jealousy," Publius says in *Federalist* 55, is a cast of mind "with which all reasoning must be vain."[8] After having argued that even under "worst-case" conditions an extended republic would protect the liberty of all Americans, Publius claims that it makes no sense to assume that such conditions will prevail. It makes no sense to assume that enlightened men will never be at the helm of government.

Publius's defense of the probability that national legislators will be enlightened statesmen rests on two points. First, to assume that the legislators will not be enlightened is to question the wisdom and ability of the American people. "I am unable to conceive that the people of America," Publius says in *Federalist* 55, "in their present temper, or under any circumstances which can speedily happen, will choose . . . men who would be disposed to form and pursue a scheme of tyranny or treachery." He makes much the same point in *Federalist* 57 when he praises "the vigilant and manly spirit which actuates the people of America—a spirit which nourishes freedom, and in return is nourished by it."[9] The Anti-Federalists, he is saying, have little faith in the people.

Second, the Anti-Federalists are also inconsistent, to Madison's way of thinking. They say they believe in republican government, yet they have a uniformly bleak view of political leadership. Their pessimism, moreover, does not square with their professed belief in civic virtue. "If men were angels, no government would be necessary," Publius says in *Federalist* 51, but in *Federalist* 55 he says that if men were the treacherous beasts that the Anti-Federalists claim, then republican government would be impossible. Publius tactfully grants that the Anti-Federalists may be "sincere friends of liberty," but points out, in impassioned tones, the contradictions of their position.

> As there is a degree of depravity in mankind which requires a certain degree of circumspection and distrust, so there are other qualities in human nature which justify a certain portion of esteem and confidence. Republican government presupposes the existence of these qualities to a higher degree than any other form. Were the pictures which have been drawn by the political jealousy of some among us faithful likenesses of the human character, the inference would be that there is not sufficient virtue among men for self-government; and that nothing less than the chains of despotism can restrain them from destroying and devouring one another.

In *Federalist* 57, Publius underscores the same issue: "What are we to say to the men who profess the most flaming zeal for republican government, yet boldly impeach the fundamental principles of it; who pretend to be champions for the right and the capacity of the people to choose their own rulers, yet maintain that they will prefer those only who will immediately and infallibly betray the trust committed to them?"[10]

Because the central task Publius faced was to dispel the Anti-Federalists' soreness, jealousy, and distrust of the Constitution, he stresses that the multiplicity of interests in an extended republic will prevent any one faction from undermining liberty, but he also accuses the Anti-Federalists of being unreasonably pessimistic about the representative process in an extended republic. Far from thinking that national legislators will become corrupted because they will not be carefully watched by their constituents, Publius thinks that those who serve in Congress will be superior in many ways to state legislators. Many Federalists had been dismayed by the kind of men who dominated in state legislatures; according to Gordon S. Wood, they "were not as much opposed to the governmental power of the states as to the character of the people who were wielding it." And Patrick Henry was right to say at the Virginia ratifying convention that "the Constitution reflects in the most degrading and mortifying manner on the virtue, integrity and wisdom of the state legislatures."[11]

Publius did not think that the men chosen to sit in a national legislature inevitably would have "more upright hearts and more enlightened minds,"[12] as Henry put it, than those who sit in state legislatures but that they would become educated by the office itself. As Madison said to Jefferson in 1787: "The most effectual remedy for the local bias" of senators or of any elected official was to impress upon their minds "an attention to the interest of the whole Society by making them the choice of the whole Society."[13] Compelled to seek votes from a wider constituency than before, candidates for congressional office would no longer be spokesmen for a narrow group of interests. And by sitting in a national legislature, congressmen would be subjected to a wide range of views on matters of public policy. The nature and responsibilities of the office would educate the man holding it. A national legislator is likely to attain a sense of what the "whole Society" requires. Madison told Jefferson that he expected that the members of a national legislature would have their own "esprit de corps."[14]

National legislators, Publius says in *Federalist* 56, should be "acquainted with the interests and circumstances" of their constituents but not bound by them.[15] For one thing, if they were confined by their pledges, then no compromises between "various and interfering interests" could take place. The representatives have to be free to negotiate between the interests they speak for and other interests. The public interest is best served by allowing representatives room in which to maneuver—enabling them, moreover, to block majority factions. The representatives then must persuade their constituents that they have gotten the best deal possible, though it might not be the deal they wanted.

But the representative, Publius argues, must do more than engage in the process of regulating "various and interfering interests" with his constituents ever in mind. He must also be willing to go directly against the wishes of his constituents when he thinks that it is in the public interest to do so, as the delegates to the Virginia ratifying convention did when they were convinced that a vote for the Constitution was in the best interest of the country. The role of the representative, then, is a difficult one. On the one hand, he is supposed to be aware of constituents' views and support those views in Congress; on the other hand, he is supposed to make his constituents aware of what he thinks is good for the country—tell them things they may not like to hear. Publius thinks that the representative must play both roles, but it is clear that the second role is the more important. He says in *Federalist* 10, weighing the advantages of different modes of representation: "By enlarging too much the number of electors, you render the representatives too little acquainted with all their local circumstances and lesser interests; as by reducing it too much, you render him unduly attached to these, and too little fit to comprehend and pursue great and national objects." In an extended republic, Publius argues, the national legislature will be composed of men capable of comprehending and pursuing "great and national objects."[16]

Publius's sense of republican government, then, is a positive one: men of "enlightened views and virtuous sentiments" will use the power they are entrusted with to advance the public good. In many ways, the political philosophy of *The Federalist* is similar to Burke's—especially to the Burke who said in "Speech to the Electors of Bristol" that Parliament "is not a *congress* of ambassadors from different and hostile interests, which interests each must maintain, as an agent and advocate, against other agents and advocates; but Parliament is a *deliberative* assembly of *one* nation, with *one* interest, that of the whole—where not local purposes, not local prejudices, ought to guide, but the general good, resulting from the general reason of the whole."[17] Publius said much the same thing in *Federalist* 57: "The aim of every political constitution is or ought to be first to obtain for rulers men who possess most wisdom to discern, and most virtue to pursue, the common good of the society. . . ."[18] Yet, many writers continue to single out *Federalists* 10 and 51 to suggest that Madison—they rarely speak of Publius—had a negative conception of representation. In *The Concept of Representation,* for example, Hannah Pitkin contrasts Madison with Burke: "Burke considers representation as a device for arriving at the right solution in Parliament and enacting it, with hopes that the people will eventually accept the action. Madison, by contrast, sees representation as a way of stalemating action in the legislature. . . ."[19] Stalemating action—or blocking majority factions—is certainly one aspect of the representative's function, but it is by no means his major one. His major function is to pursue "great and national objects."

In a sense, Publius's national legislature, chosen by the people, is a more self-contained deliberative body than Burke's Parliament, where many members were honor bound to support the policies of those who found them a seat. American representatives have no obligation other than to pursue the public interest. Although sovereignty lies in the people, authority lies in the legislature. As Publius says in *Federalist* 63, the distinctive nature of American republican government *"lies in the total exclusion of the people in their collective capacity"*[20] from any sharing in the government. For Publius, then, Congress is an independent body, beholden to no one. The extent of the representative's duty to his constituents is only that he be acquainted with their interests and therefore at least take them into consideration when he engages in deliberation.

Burke and Publius agree, in general, about the role of national legislators, but they disagree about how such legislators should be chosen. Publius was a republican; Burke was not. In Publius's view, the legitimacy of Congress derives from the American people, who elect its members. The people do not participate in deliberation, but they are central to the political process. Burke, by contrast, had little faith in the English people's ability to choose wise leaders, and he wanted to restrict even further a franchise that was more limited than the American one. Burke's Parliament, which derives its legitimacy not from the British people but from the British Constitution, is an assembly chosen by an elite, an assembly of men who for the most part are placed in office by a system of "influence" that was abhorred by virtually all Americans, Federalists and Anti-Federalists alike. The British system may have made it easier, as Burke thought, for intelligent, public-spirited men to find their way into politics, but it was a system that violated republican principles, a system of which Publius did not approve.

But there is one more sense in which Publius is a Burkean. Like Burke, Publius thinks it wrong to assume that those who aspire to office—those, that is, who seek office rather than have it thrust upon them—are generally driven by a lust for power. For both Burke and Publius, the political vocation is an honorable one, and Burke would have agreed with Publius when he attacked the Anti-Federalists for their bleak view of political leaders. As Burke himself asked in "Letter to the Sheriffs of Bristol": "If all men who act in a public situation are equally selfish, corrupt, and venal, what reason can be given for desiring any sort of change, which besides the evils which must attend all changes, can be productive of no possible advantage?"[21] Both Burke and Publius thought it foolish to assume that political leaders would always be corrupted by power. Impatient with the fears of the Anti-Federalists, Madison proclaimed at the Virginia ratifying convention: "I go on this great republican principle, that the people will have virtue and intelligence to select men of virtue and wisdom. Is there no virtue among us? If there be not, we are in a wretched situation. No theoretical checks, no form of government, can render us secure. To suppose that any form of government will secure liberty or happiness without any virtue in the people, is a chimerical idea."[22] Republican government will fail, Madison says, if it is incapable of electing men of civic virtue as national legislators. But he was hopeful that national legislators would generally pursue "great and national objects."

For Publius as well as Burke the political vocation requires courage as well as civic virtue—the mettle to go against the wishes of one's constituents. In *Federalists* 63 and 71, Publius argues that legislators at times must ignore public opinion. "The republican principle," he states in *Federalist* 71,

> demands that the deliberate sense of the community should govern the conduct of those to whom they intrust the management of their affairs; but it does not require an unqualified complaisance to every sudden breeze of passion, or to every transient impulse which the people may receive from the arts of men, who flatter their prejudices to betray their interests. . . . When occasions present themselves in which the interests of the people are at variance with their inclinations, it is the duty of the persons whom they have appointed to be the guardians of those interests to withstand the temporary delusion in order to give them time and opportunity for more cool and sedate reflection.

Those who thus serve their constituents "at the peril of their displeasure," Publius adds, are men of "courage and magnanimity," men whose conduct "has saved the people from [the] very fatal consequences of their own mistakes. . . ."[23]

Federalist 71 was written by Hamilton, and perhaps it makes the point about a courageous legislator more strongly than his chief collaborator would have liked. Madison is usually more careful to qualify his defense of the legislator by saying, as he does in *Federalist* 57, for example, that "effectual precautions" must be taken for keeping legislators "virtuous whilst they continue to hold their public trust."[24] One historian has called Publius a split personality: Madison as the defender of negative government (a government that prevents majority faction) pulling in one direction, and Hamilton as an apostle of positive government (a government in which legislators undertake "extensive and arduous enterprises for the public benefit") pulling in the other.[25] Perhaps so, but in *The Federalist* they both wore the mask of Publius, and it is difficult to say where Madison's ideas leave off and Hamilton's begin. (We are not even sure of the authorship of several *Federalist* papers.) True, Hamilton and Madison were only temporary allies. They would soon go their separate ways, but in 1787 and 1788 they worked hard to get the Constitution ratified even though they were in many ways dissatisfied with it, because they thought that if it was not ratified the country would fall apart. As Publius says of all those who approved the Constitution: "All the deputies composing the convention were either satisfactorily accommodated by the final act, or were induced to accede to it by a deep conviction of the necessity of sacrificing private opinions and partial interests to the public good, and by a despair of seeing this necessity diminished by delays or by new experiments."[26]

In 1812 Jefferson said of Madison, "I do not know in the world a man of purer integrity, more dispassionate, disinterested, and devoted to genuine Republicanism."[27] The same may be said of Hamilton. According to Richard Morris, "Hamilton was without question the least affluent man in American history to hold the office of Secretary of the Treasury. He did not enter public service to make money, and he never made any out of it. This was explicit in letters written from the days of the Revolution."[28] But in one sense neither man was disinterested. La Rochefoucauld often suggests in his maxims that we should not understand by self-interest a concern only with money and wealth; self-interest often takes the form of a desire for fame and glory. Insofar as Madison and Hamilton were both animated by a love of fame, they were driven by self-interest. "The love of fame," Publius says in *Federalist* 72, is "the ruling passion of the noblest minds. . . ."[29] Douglass Adair asserts that "the desire for fame operated . . . as a constant goad in the political behavior of the mature Washington, of Adams, of Jefferson, Hamilton, and Madison."[30]

For Madison and Hamilton the love of fame is closely connected with civic virtue. They would have agreed with Dante that "contempt of fame begets contempt of virtue."[31] Most Americans, as we have seen, thought otherwise. They still worried, as they had in colonial times, about false patriots, those who "under a show of public spirit and zeal for the liberties of their country"[32] are actually bent upon arrogating limitless power to themselves and subverting liberty. Madison and Hamilton acknowledged that ambition can take sinister forms, but "opposed to the corrupting tendencies of power the sobering influence of responsibility."[33] Trying to persuade the Anti-Federalists that power does not always lead to the betrayal of public trust, Publius argues in *Federalist* 57 that "those ties which bind the representative to his constituents are strengthened by motives of a more *selfish* nature. His pride and vanity attach him to a form of government which favors his pretensions and gives him a share in its honors and distinctions" (emphasis added).[34] Both Hamilton and Madison attempted, if only fitfully, because their main concern was practical affairs rather than political theory, to rethink the question of the relation of disinterest to self-interest. In their other writing, as well as in *The Federalist,* they imply that there is not necessarily a chasm between self-interested conduct and disinterested conduct. Self-interest in fame and glory can prod a man to act as a disinterested legislator. Or as Douglass Adair put it, "The love of fame is a noble passion because it can transform ambition and self-interest into a dedicated effort for the community. . . ."[35]

Preoccupied with preserving the health of the republic, Madison and Hamilton were close to the tradition of civic humanism, which arose in the late Middle Ages and culminated in the work of Machiavelli and Guicciardini. Quentin Skinner relates that Florentine civic humanism was devoted "not merely to upholding the central value of Republican liberty, but also to analyzing the causes of its vulnerability"[36] in order to recommend the best methods for ensuring the health of the Republic. The Florentine civic humanists were devoted, as were the authors of *The Federalist,* to finding republican remedies "for the diseases most incident to republican government."

Like Hamilton and Madison, the Florentine civic humanists thought that sovereignty resided in the people. And, like Hamilton and Madison, the Florentine civic humanists considered a knowledge of rhetoric essential to those entering public life. Finally, like Hamilton and Madison, the Florentine civic humanists thought a career in public life the most honorable career possible. According to Machiavelli, honor and fame accrue to those "who have gone to the trouble of serving their country,"[37] to those who possess "virtù," a word that was translated in a late-seventeenth-century edition of Machiavelli's works as "public spirit."

In their attitude toward special interests, however, Hamilton and Madison differ from Machiavelli and most of the Florentine civic humanists. According to Machiavelli, a concern with one's private interests and a failure to devote one's energies to the common good are signs of corruption, and the prevalence of corruption leads to the collapse of republican government. By contrast, Madison and Hamilton, writing as Publius, praised private interest. But the difference between Machiavelli and Publius is not as great as it may seem. According to Madison and Hamilton, there are essentially two kinds of men: those animated by an interest in their own economic concerns and those animated by an interest in fame and glory. Because they thought the rise of commerce would lead to political stability, they encouraged the growth of the first class of people, but they assumed that the country would always be governed by the second class—by men whose desire for fame leads them to dedicate their lives to public service, by men who recognize what George F. Will has called "the dignity of the political vocation and the grandeur of its responsibilities."[38] These men would not be a governing class by virtue of their social or economic status in private life, as Burke's legislators were. Rather, they would be a "natural aristocracy," as Jefferson said to Madison. Coming from different backgrounds and walks of life, they would be transformed by sitting in a national legislature into a body of men, Publius says in *Federalist* 10, "whose wisdom may best discern the true interest of the country, and whose patriotism and love of justice will be least likely to sacrifice it to temporary or partial considerations."[39]

These men, then, would be patriots, but they would practice a new kind of patriotism. At the Constitutional Convention, Hamilton had said that "a reliance on pure patriotism [was] the source of many of our errors."[40] The new kind of patriotism was an alloy—a patriotism that was more flexible and generous than the patriotism of the Anti-Federalists, a patriotism that was public-spirited without being high-minded, a patriotism tempered by the principles of the science of politics. Versed in the principles of the science of politics, the new kind of patriot would acknowledge the legitimacy of "various and interfering interests," would refrain from attacking the motives of those who disagreed with him, and would prefer deliberation to declamation.

The new kind of patriotism adumbrated in *The Federalist,* however, is Publius's vision—not the vision of Hamilton and Madison. It was not that Hamilton and Madison had simply concocted a scheme that they thought would help to gain support for ratification. Rather, it was that in private Hamilton and Madison were less sanguine that this new kind of patriotism could be put into effect. At the Constitutional Convention, Madison had spoken candidly about the grave sectional division that existed between slaveholding and nonslaveholding states. "The great division of interests in the United States," he records himself as saying, does not "lie between large and small States [but] between the Northern and Southern."[41] Thus Madison thought there was not a "multiplicity of interests" but only two great interests, and in 1789 he confessed to a friend that the votes of northern congressmen already confirmed the Anti-Federalists' warning that the North might become a majority faction inimical to the rights and interests of the South.

Madison and Hamilton also were less sanguine than Publius that parties from principle would give way to parties from interest. The science of politics was based on the hope that the rise of commerce would make factions based on different opinions an increasingly rare phenomenon. Yet, as John Plamenatz asserts, "Interests common to large numbers of people are nearly always put forward in the shape of principles," and "men acquire new interests largely because they acquire new principles. . . ."[42] Opinion may govern interest, but opinion and interest are often inextricable. Yet, if parties continue to be parties from principle—parties governed by different opinions—it will be difficult for national legislators to regulate "various and interfering interests." When Publius says that the new American government will function smoothly because there will be a multiplicity of interests, he is expressing a hope rather than a strong conviction—the hope of a

Federalist trying to reassure the Anti-Federalists that the new Constitution is definitely the lesser evil. In private, Madison and Hamilton were still worried that the Republic might be afflicted, as most republics had been, with different parties from principle; in private, they were still worried about the possibility of violent civic discord.

So much for Publius's model. But was it a model that was accurate? Has American politics worked according to the way Publius envisioned it would work? In one sense, clearly it has not. Publius assumed that different interests would continually shift to block the formation of majority factions. What he did not envision was the formation of political parties. As Richard Hofstadter makes clear: "The Founding Fathers did not have, in their current experience or historical knowledge, models of working parties that would have encouraged them to think in such terms. First, parties had to be created; and then at last they would begin to find a theoretical acceptance."[43]

Perhaps more important, neither Madison nor Hamilton, of course, knew that within five years they would become bitter enemies—not merely the spokesmen for different parties from interest but the spokesmen for two political parties. The parties of the 1790s, however, were not parties as we know them now; they were parties from principle—parties that regarded each other as subversive, as threatening the very life of the Republic. In the 1790s, opinion clearly triumphed over interest—casting into doubt the notions that informed Madison's and Hamilton's science of politics as well as severely threatening the workings of the new American republic. In the second half of this essay, we will examine not only the politics of the 1790s but also the politics of the Gilded Age and the 1970s both to assess whether Publius's model—despite its omission of political parties—is at all helpful as a guide to American politics and to gauge in general the influence of special interests on American politics.

Notes

1. John Patrick Diggins, "Power and Authority in American History: The Case of Charles A. Beard and His Critics," *American Historical Review* 86 (1981):702.
2. Cited, Douglass Adair, *Fame and the Founding Fathers,* ed. Trevor Colbourn (New York: W. W. Norton, 1974), p. 86n.
3. David Truman, *The Governmental Process* (New York: Alfred A. Knopf, 1971), p. 509.
4. Kenneth Morgan, "Madison's Theory of Representation in the Tenth Federalist," *Journal of Politics* 36 (1974):881.
5. Clinton Rossiter, ed., *The Federalist Papers* (New York: New American Library, 1961), p. 80.
6. Ibid., p. 82.

7. Ibid., p. 83.
8. Ibid., p. 345.
9. Ibid., pp. 344, 353.
10. Ibid., pp. 346, 353.
11. Gordon Wood, *The Creation of the American Republic, 1776–1787* (New York: W. W. Norton, 1972), p. 507; cited, ibid.
12. Ibid.
13. Cited, ibid., p. 511.
14. Ibid., p. 505.
15. Rossiter, *Federalist Papers,* p. 346.
16. Ibid., p. 83.
17. *Edmund Burke on Government, Politics, and Society,* ed. B. W. Hill (New York: International Publications Service, 1970), p. 158.
18. Rossiter, *Federalist Papers,* p. 350.
19. Hannah Pitkin, *The Concept of Representation* (Berkeley: University of California Press, 1967), p. 196.
20. Rossiter, *Federalist Papers,* p. 387.
21. *Edmund Burke: Selected Works,* ed. W. J. Bate (New York: Random House, 1960), p. 221.
22. Cited, Alexander Landi, "Madison's Political Theory," *Political Science Review* 6 (1976):108.
23. Rossiter, *Federalist Papers,* p. 432.
24. Ibid., p. 350.
25. Alpheus T. Mason, "*The Federalist*—A Split Personality," in *Origins of American Political Thought,* ed. John P. Roche (New York: Harper & Row, 1967), pp. 163–92.
26. Rossiter, *Federalist Papers,* p. 231.
27. Cited, Irving Brant, *The Fourth President: A Life of James Madison* (Indianapolis: Bobbs-Merrill, 1970), p. 44.
28. *The Basic Ideas of Alexander Hamilton,* ed. Richard B. Morris (New York: Pocket Books, 1957), p. 433.
29. Rossiter, *Federalist Papers,* p. 437.
30. Adair, *Fame and the Founding Fathers,* p. 24.
31. Cited, ibid., p. 11n.
32. Cited, Bernard Bailyn, *The Origins of American Politics* (New York: Alfred A. Knopf, 1968), p. 140n.
33. Gerald Stourzh, *Alexander Hamilton and the Idea of Republican Government* (Stanford: Stanford University Press, 1970), p. 180.
34. Rossiter, *Federalist Papers,* p. 352.
35. Adair, *Fame and the Founding Fathers,* p. 12.
36. Quentin Skinner, *The Foundations of Modern Political Thought,* vol. 1: *The Renaissance* (Cambridge: Cambridge University Press, 1978), p. 41.
37. Cited, ibid., p. 176.
38. George F. Will, *The Pursuit of Happiness and Other Sobering Thoughts* (New York: Harper & Row, 1978), p. xvi.
39. Rossiter, *Federalist Papers,* p. 82.
40. Cited, Stourzh, *Alexander Hamilton,* p. 84.
41. Cited, Brant, *Fourth President,* p. 168.
42. John Plamenatz, *Man and Society,* vol. 1 (London: Longman, 1963), pp. 321–22.
43. Richard Hofstadter, *The Idea of a Party System* (Berkeley: University of California Press, 1970), p. 39.

PART II

THE WORKINGS OF A SCIENCE OF POLITICS

It is impossible to take politics out of politics.
—Thomas Corcoran

4

The 1790s: Monocrats and Jacobins

In the years that immediately followed the ratification of the Constitution and the inauguration of George Washington, the "multiplicity of interests" that Publius had hoped could be "regulated" in an extended republic arranged themselves, broadly speaking, into two distinct interests: the commercial North and the agricultural South. Hamilton, as Washington's secretary of the treasury, became the leader of the former, and Madison, the Speaker of the House of Representatives, the leader of the latter, though "leader" may be a misleading term for men who were the chief publicists for factions that soon became the Federalist party and the Republican party. Publius no longer existed. The two men, who had cooperated on what would eventually be regarded as a classic text of American political theory, became—in the unseemly space of less than five years—bitter enemies. They regarded each other not merely as spokesmen for different interests but as leaders of forces that threatened the new Republic. In the 1790s opinion—not interest—held sway, opinion in the form of opposing views about the French Revolution. Such views could easily breed factional violence.

Before the French Revolution cast its shadow over American politics, however, "regulation" did take place. As a spokesman for the agricultural South, Madison acknowledged that his section's interests constrained him to disagree with Hamilton on questions of national fiscal policy, but he thought that such differences could be worked out on the basis of "mutual concessions" in the interest of the national welfare. In 1789, therefore, he proposed a mercantilist policy of tonnage duties that would place a disproportionate financial burden on his region. Such measures, he argued, were necessary to transform the United States into a commercial, manufacturing, and maritime power. As the sponsor of a bill that would primarily benefit the North's commercial and maritime interests, he hoped to dispel the strong notion—rife both in the North and the South—that the two regions were inevitably bound to clash on most matters because their interests were so far apart.

Madison's bill had one feature that was a portent of the more profound discord that would jar the 1790s: a section of it provided for discrimination against the ships and merchandise of foreign countries that had no commercial treaties with the United States. If this section of the bill were passed, France would benefit at Britain's expense because the United States had concluded a commercial treaty with France in 1778. Madison thought such a shift in trade would reduce American dependence upon Britain, but most northerners feared that American commerce could ill afford to wage economic warfare with Great Britain. The bill was passed without the section, but it increased the suspicion with which the two regions of the country regarded each other. Hamilton, who was still a private citizen practicing law in New York, thought that Madison and his friends were less interested in the financial health of the United States than in pursuing a policy of revenge against Britain. And many southerners feared that northern interests were fast becoming a majority faction against which the agricultural South would have little recourse.

Southern fears increased dramatically during the next two years as Hamilton, the new secretary of the treasury, unveiled his fiscal policy. His recommendations appeared in a series of reports submitted to Congress in 1790 and 1791: *Report on Public Credit, Recommendation for Establishing a Bank of the United States,* and *Report on Manufactures.* An exponent of "energy" in government, Hamilton favored a strong national fiscal policy that would foster industrialization. Such a policy would enable the United States to survive in a world of increasingly restrictive mercantilist systems. It was a policy, moreover, designed both to attract foreign capital and to promote the development of manufacturing, for Hamilton thought Americans were overly inclined to invest their capital in land speculation, shipping, and merchandising. He realized that his recommendations would immediately redound to the benefit of the North, but argued that the economy of the nation was indivisible and that in the long run all branches would benefit from "a universal vivification of the energies of industry."[1] If manufacturing were developed, then southern raw materials would travel to northern factories. Commerce would flow between the two regions rather than in a transatlantic direction, and divisional jealousies would disappear. The South as well as the North, Hamilton argued, would benefit from his policies.

Southerners, especially Virginians, did not agree. During the debate on *Report on Public Credit,* Senator Richard Lee of Virginia decided that he would prefer dissolution of the Union to "the rule of a fixed insolent northern majority."[2] And Patrick Henry, who had said that the Constitution was a plot concocted by the North to dominate the South, was honored in Virginia as a prophet whose warnings had not been taken seriously. If Henry Lee overstated his case when he said that Hamilton's measure might "produce ruin" for Virginia, there was no question that the North would immediately reap the rewards. Because more than four-fifths of the national debt was owed to citizens living north of the Mason-Dixon line, many southerners objected that the funding and assumption measures proposed in *Report on Public Credit* would result in their taxes lining the pockets of northern financial speculators. Hamilton tried to convince southerners that even though more northerners would gain from the measures, he was not simply trying to promote northern interests. But he was not persuasive enough, and Madison found himself constrained to oppose strenuously most of the recommendations of his recent close collaborator, going so far as to question the constitutionality of some of the measures. As for Hamilton, he considered Madison's opposition on the question of public credit as "a perfidious desertion of the principles which he [Madison] was solemnly pledged to defend."[3]

The South may have been unhappy with Hamilton's proposals, but many southerners—including Madison and Jefferson—were still disposed to work toward a compromise that would meet some of their interests. Consequently, Jefferson and Madison agreed to muster congressional support for Hamilton's funding-assumption plan provided Hamilton agreed to the new capital's being established on the Potomac rather than in New York. Both sides made concessions. Hamilton's was bound to antagonize those New Yorkers who had expected their city to be the capital, especially because fifty thousand dollars had already been expended upon the construction of a federal hall. Jefferson and Madison, in turn, were backing measures that would be extremely unpopular in their state. Somewhat modified, the bill concerning funding-assumption passed by a narrow margin, as did a bill concerning the establishment of a Bank of the United States. Finally, many of the recommendations made by Hamilton in *Report on Manufactures* were incorporated in the Tariff Act of May 1792.

Despite strong sectional differences, then, "regulation" did take place. Congressional politics during Washington's first term of office may not have conformed exactly to Publius's model of a scientific politics based on a multiplicity of interests, but at least the leaders of the two sectional interests realized the need for accommodation. The language of the patriotic tradition, however, still remained a vital strain in American politics. Questioning Hamilton's *Report on Public Credit,* Patrick Henry asked in 1790: "When the systems of the vilest and most corrupt government find advocates in the councils of America, shall we dare any longer to say that America is the land of freedom?"[4] Such rhetoric, however, would not have been effective were it not for the French Revolution, which became a significant factor in American politics by 1793.

The French Revolution acted as a catalyst, transforming a quarrel between sectional interests into a quarrel between factions that regarded each other as subversive. As the decade progressed, the party of Madison came to regard the opposition less as simply the spokesmen for the interests of the commercial North than as a British party—a party, that is, so enamored of Britain that it wished to set up an American government along British lines. And the party of Hamilton, in turn, came to see the opposition less as the spokesmen for the interests of the agricultural South than as the French party—a party, that is, so enthusiastic about the French Revolution that it encouraged a Jacobin conspiracy to introduce French despotism and atheism into the United States. The Federalist party and the Republican party arose out of differences of interest, but the effect of the French Revolution was to change them into parties that were volatile mixtures of opinion and interest, with opinion clearly being the dominant factor. In Hume's terms, they became parties from principle rather than parties from interest. Because each party questioned the republican faith of the other, accommodation by means of mutual concessions became virtually impossible. As a result, during the rest of the decade American politics gave few signs of working according to Publius's model.

The French Revolution came to loom large in American affairs in spite of the resolution of Congress to "be as little as possible entangled in the politics and controversies of European nations."[5] Publius had endorsed such feelings, but he was not sanguine that the Old World would leave the New alone. "Though a wide ocean separates the United States from Europe," he says in *Federalist* 24, "yet there are various considerations that warn against an excess of confidence or security." Publius, in fact, was concerned that the blatant weaknesses of the central government under the Articles of Confederation constituted a standing invitation for European powers to meddle in American affairs. "Let Americans disdain to be instruments of European greatness!" he declaims at the close of *Federalist* 11. "Let the thirteen States, bound together in a strict and indissoluble Union, concur in erecting one great American system superior to the control of all transatlantic force or influence and able to dictate the terms of the connection between the old and the new world!" In calling for a strong central government, Publius implies that the United States to some extent had to practice a foreign policy similar to that of other "corrupt" nations. It had, that is, to pursue its "true interest" in a rational and realistic manner. And it could effectively pursue that interest only if its threat of force were credible. Warning that under the current government a European war would probably wreak havoc on American shipping, Publius in *Federalist*

41 says that "security against foreign danger . . . is an avowed and essential object of the American Union."[6]

Federalist 41 was written by Madison, but of the two principal collaborators it was Hamilton who was especially interested in matters of foreign policy, and the majority of the Publius essays on the subject can be ascribed to him. Well versed in the extensive eighteenth-century literature on the interests of states, doctrines that usually espoused the notion that a brutal struggle for power determined the relationship between countries, Hamilton thought American foreign policy should be conducted along traditional European lines, which meant above all that Americans should not be swayed by their republican sentiments to pursue a foreign policy that might be harmful to the nation's "true interest." Hamilton, of course, was aware that many Americans still hated Great Britain, but he thought such sentiments should not prevent the Washington administration from cultivating close commercial ties with its former enemy. Because most American trade was with Britain, Hamilton reasoned that any attempt to make France the chief trading partner of the United States would be disastrous to domestic economic development; France would never be an adequate market for American raw materials. Such a policy would risk the flight of British capital, which was desperately needed, Hamilton believed, to bolster industrial development. Moreover, Britain was a greater naval power than France, and therefore it would be foolish to risk war with her by courting France. According to Hamilton, the United States had more to gain than lose by cultivating good relations with its former enemy. Madison saw things otherwise: American dependence on British trade was excessive and unhealthy, and war with Britain was highly improbable.

No doubt, even if the French Revolution had not occurred, Hamilton and Madison would have parted ways because they were spokesmen for different sections of the country. But it was the French Revolution that eventually turned them into implacable enemies. Before the French Revolution, whether the true interest of the United States lay in close ties with France or Britain was, to some degree, an emotionally neutral question, though sentiment perhaps leaned toward France because of its aid during the revolutionary war. But after the French Revolution—and especially after France became a republic in 1792—the question became laden with emotional intensity. Increasingly, Americans became Republicans or Federalists less because of their different interests—it was often not clear, in any case, which policies would benefit which interests—than because of their opinions about developments in France. As Richard Buel, Jr., comments: "Although the perception of economic interest did influence the politics of many individuals and some regions, it does not provide a comprehensive explanation for party alignments."[7] Because the news from France—indeed, from all of Europe—changed dramatically as the decade progressed, and because the conduct of both the French and British governments with respect to the United States also changed dramatically, party alignments were remarkably fluid during the middle years of the decade. The 1790s were a decade of violent oscillations in public opinion.

The year 1792 was the watershed. Parties then "did not reach very deeply into the political life of the country,"[8] but the language of political debate was definitely becoming infected with allegations that Hamilton's faction was a British party and Madison's faction a French party. In his political broadside, "Spirit of Governments," published in February 1792, Madison virtually accuses Hamilton of trying to turn the Republic into a government that closely resembled Britain's. Madison distinguishes among three kinds of governments: the first, "a government operating by a permanent military force"; the second, "a government operating by corrupt influence"; and the third, "a government deriving its energy from the will of society," a republican government "which it is the glory of America to have invented, and her unrivalled happiness to possess." But it is the second kind, Madison implies, that Hamilton has in mind, given his fiscal policies. The extent of Madison's fears about Hamilton's intentions can be gauged by the language he uses to describe the second kind of government; he speaks of it as a government that substitutes "the motive of private interest in place of public duty," a government that accommodates "its measures to the avidity of a part of the nation instead of the benefit of the whole. . . ."[9] Attacking private interest now, Madison jettisons the notions that form the basis of *Federalists* 10 and 51, and resorts to the patriotic rhetoric that he had thought would result in violent factions.

What, we may wonder, has happened to the Madison who wore the mask of Publius, the Madison of *The Federalist?* Madison's inconsistency is understandable if we keep in mind that for Publius the regulation of "various and interfering interests" could take place only if there were a multiplicity of interests, no one much more powerful than another. But Madison was convinced that Hamilton's policies were fast leading to the creation of "a large monied interest" that would permanently control the country. "No lines can be laid down for civil or political wisdom," Burke asserts in "Thoughts on The Cause of the Present Discontents,"[10] by which he means that the wise and prudent politician should always take into account the nature of the particular situation. Madison, who was first and foremost a politician rather than a political theorist, would have agreed. In 1787, he had devoted much time to writing essays in support of ratifying the Constitution because he feared that without a strong central government the Republic would fall into anarchy. In 1792, however, it was the spectre of tyranny, not anarchy, that disturbed him; he thought the country in danger of being taken over by a minority faction of plutocrats whose commitment to republican government was frail at best. The new danger to the Republic required a political stance very different from the one he had taken five years earlier.

Madison claims in "A Candid State of Parties" (published in September 1792) that the new danger required the formation of a strong party. Only such a party could effectively combat what he calls an anti-Republican party composed of men who hoped to keep themselves forever in power by strengthening themselves with "the men of influence, particularly of moneyed, which is the most active and insinuating influence."[11] A manifesto for the new Republican party—or, as many congressmen called it in 1792, Mr. Madison's party—Madison's essay was not, however, a manifesto in favor of parties, for Madison regarded Hamilton's party as illegitimate.

Madison, of course, endeavored to persuade his fellow congressmen to vote against Hamilton's proposals, but he had given up any hope of persuading Hamilton to change his views. In January 1793, Madison voted in favor of a ten-point indictment of Hamilton's conduct as secretary of the treasury, by which he hoped to force his resignation. Because the indictment, which was drafted by Jefferson, was defeated by a considerable majority, it is hard to agree with Madison's assertion in "A Candid State of Parties" that the so-called anti-Republicans were "weaker in point of numbers."[12] Such may have been the case in the country at large, but it was not the case in Congress. Yet, the very fact that Madison could make such a claim shows that the lines were being drawn, that by the close of 1792 congressmen had begun to take sides, seeing themselves as either Republicans or Federalists. The party alignments, it should be stressed, did not clearly conform to regional interests, though Virginia was the stronghold of the Republicans and New England the stronghold of the Federalists.

Hamilton, on his part, was bewildered and disturbed by Madison's opposition. He could find no reason for it except to suggest, in a letter of May 1792, that Madison's loyalty to the Union was weak. Madison's attachment to the government of the United States, Hamilton said, is "more an affair of the head than of the heart; more the result of a conviction of the necessity of Union than of cordiality to the thing itself." Madison was a passionate Virginian rather than a passionate Unionist, and he was in league with men who "deem it expedient to risk rendering the government itself odious."[13] Yet, if the partisans of the states succeed in weakening the national government, Hamilton suggests, public strength and private security will suffer, and the Republic will descend into faction and anarchy. Only demagogues, he concludes, stand to benefit from the disorder that Madison's policies will produce.

Hamilton, moreover, swears that there is no substance to the rumors that there exists "a monarchical party meditating the destruction of . . . republican government."[14] The subverters of republican government, he claims, are Madison and his followers. Madison, as we have seen, made the same claims about Hamilton and his followers. In another letter written in 1792, Hamilton describes the differences between the two parties: "One side appears to believe that there is a serious plot to overturn the State governments, and substitute a monarchy to the present republican system. The other side firmly believes that there is a serious plot to overturn the general government and elevate the separate powers of the States upon its ruins." Both sides, Hamilton concludes in a remarkably cool-headed assessment, "may be equally wrong. . . ."[15] The events of 1793, however, would make such a dispassionate analysis of American politics an increasingly rare phenomenon.

In January 1793, France beheaded Louis XVI. In February it declared war upon Great Britain and appointed Citizen Edmund Genêt minister to the United States. As a result of these actions, and events related to them, France became the central question of American politics, one that would prove bitterly divisive in the course of the next five years. In 1792, Hamilton had thought the politics of Madison's party foolish and potentially subversive, confiding to a friend that Madison and Jefferson "have a womanish attachment to France and a womanish resentment against Great Britain."[16] By the close of 1793, he and other Federalists were thinking that Madison's and Jefferson's politics bordered upon the treasonous. Recent events, Jefferson said to Monroe in June 1793, have "kindled and brought forward the two parties with an ardour which our own interests merely, could never excite."[17] Opinion held sway over interest.

In 1793 the majority of Americans favored France. Even in Britain, the war with France was generally unpopular, and hated by a vocal minority that was vehemently hostile to the ministry and the Parliament. In the United States, pro-French feeling was even stronger, and it was not confined to the South. In 1793, the pastor of a congregation in Plymouth, Massachusetts, using abundant quotations from the Bible, pronounced a eulogy of the French Revolution, and in 1794, the Massachusetts Historical Society resolved that the happiness of "the whole world of Mankind" depended on the success of the French Revolution.[18] Even Noah Webster, who was a moderate Federalist, spoke of the European coalition against France as "a vile league of tyrants."[19] Throughout 1793 elaborate civic festivals in honor of France were held throughout the country. To many Americans, France's war with Britain bore a close resemblance to their own revolutionary war; it was a struggle that set liberty against tyranny, republicanism against monarchy.

Worried that the strong swell of pro-French enthusiasm might lead to a war with Britain, Hamilton in April 1793 persuaded Washington to issue a neutrality proclamation stating that the United States intended to pursue "a conduct friendly and impartial towards the belligerent powers."[20] The notion of impartiality stuck in the throat of Madison's party, and Madison himself—under the pen name Helvidius—argued that Congress controlled foreign policy, and that the powers of the president in the diplomatic field were instrumental only. Madison also said that the proclamation was inconsistent with the stated treaty obligations to France of the United States. Such positions convinced Hamilton that Madison and his followers were bent on a course designed to abet the French by provoking a war with Britain, a course that he thought would be disastrous to the United States.

Hamilton was wrong; Madison and Jefferson—as well as most responsible Republicans—did not want war with Britain. They did think, however, that the "true interest" of the United States lay in maintaining friendly relations with France, even if by doing so it would antagonize Britain. Such a policy, they thought, was based on an eminently realistic assessment of the situation in Europe. Even if provoked, Britain could not risk another war with the United States, for it was on the verge of financial ruin and there was a good deal of internal disorder and opposition to the current government. Jefferson especially was certain that the British monarchy would soon collapse. The logic of history, he thought, was on the side of republican France, and French successes on the battlefield in 1794 only confirmed his views. Even if France were not as strong as it appeared to be, it was in the United States' interest to support it as a first line of defense against tyranny, for if the Coalition defeated France, it might go on to attack the United States, a sister republic.

The party of Hamilton, of course, thought otherwise. France, Hamilton argued, was the weaker of the two countries because its government—not Britain's—was unstable. The French Revolution was far from showing "the same dignity, the same solemnity, which distinguished the course of the American Revolution"; instead, "passion, tumult, and violence" were "usurping those seats, where reason and cool deliberation ought to preside."[21] France would soon descend into anarchy and civil violence, only to be rescued from chaos by a despot. A policy that might provoke a war with France, Hamilton thought, was less dangerous to the United States, because—owing to imminent internal collapse—France did not constitute a serious threat to the United States. A war with Britain, however, would be ruinous to American shipping and would also "arrest the present rapid progress to strength and prosperity."[22] According to the party of Hamilton, the United States could not risk antagonizing Britain.

The arguments propounded by both parties were not simply strategic, not simply a question of estimating the relative strengths of Britain and

France in order to determine which was more dangerous to offend. For the parties, strategy and morality were intimately related. Hamilton and his followers thought the French regime immoral insofar as it was based on atheistical principles—principles that were fundamentally antithetical to republican government and ultimately destructive of American society. Madison and his followers thought the British regime immoral because it was not only a monarchy but also a regime based on corruption and privilege. As Richard Hofstadter explains: "Each party saw the other as having a foreign allegiance, British or French, that approached the edge of treason. Each also saw the other as having a political aspiration or commitment that lay outside the republican covenant of the Constitution: the Federalists were charged with being 'Monocrats,' with aspiring to restore monarchy and the hereditary principle; the Republicans with advocating a radical, French-inspired democracy hostile to property and order."[23]

Unfortunately, there was some basis to the charges of foreign influence. Both Hamilton and Jefferson were notoriously indiscreet in the way they shared confidences with either English or French ambassadors. In 1790, Hamilton had offered the English ambassador arguments with which to combat Jefferson with regard to drawing up a commercial treaty with Great Britain. And in 1793 Jefferson himself foolishly took Citizen Genêt into his confidence, warning him about Hamilton and his partisans. Citizen Genêt became so certain that the American people objected to Washington's policy against French privateering that he called for a special session of Congress so that the representatives of the people could judge between the president of the United States and the minister of the French republic. Such interference in American politics was too much even for Jefferson, and he acquiesced in Hamilton's recommendation that France recall its ambassador.

Citizen Genêt's stormy diplomatic career ended abruptly toward the close of 1793 when the Jacobins, having consolidated their power over the Girondists, ordered him to return to France to stand trial for "criminal maneuvers." (He chose to remain in the United States.) The question of foreign influence, however, continued to bedevil American politics for the next four years, affecting the course of the Jay Treaty, a commercial treaty with Britain that was strongly opposed by Republicans, ratified by the Senate in July 1795 and then signed by the president. In the House Madison attempted to neutralize it by proposing legislation that would prevent the expenditure of funds needed for its implementation. After a dramatic debate on 28 April 1796, the bill carrying the treaty into execution was passed by the narrow margin of 51 to 48.

Because the treaty resulted in a close trading relationship with Britain, it was clearly a triumph of Federalist policy. It was not, however, a popular treaty. Pro-French feeling still remained very strong, and after the terms of the treaty were leaked to the press in 1795 the administration was accused of betraying American interests and of linking the United States with the "Caligula of Great Britain." John Jay was burned in effigy throughout the country and a Boston town meeting condemned the treaty without even reading it. In New York, Hamilton was pelted with stones while trying to defend it. Even rich merchants, whose interest lay in having close ties with Britain, disapproved of it. To many Americans, the treaty was proof that Hamilton and his followers were completely under the influence of the British monarchy. And John Jay's conduct while he was in Britain to negotiate the treaty—he had praised George III's "justice and benevolence" and he had prided himself upon having none of the "ancient Prejudices"[24] that might stand in the way of a settlement—made such charges plausible.

If British influence on Washington's administration became a matter of controversy, French influence suddenly became a very serious problem to Washington himself. Late in 1795, Washington was shocked to learn that Edmund Randolph, his secretary of state, had been engaged in an intrigue with the French minister to the United States. Captured documents divulged by the British revealed that at the least Randolph had served as a conduit for French bribes to American politicians. Randolph may not have been guilty of treason, but he was compromised to such a degree that he had to resign. And Washington, worried that French influence was rife in the highest councils of government, decided despite some reservations to sign the Jay Treaty. The fear of French influence had impelled Washington to establish close ties with Britain.

Yet Washington did not want to provoke a war with France. As the American ambassador to France, James Monroe was supposed to reassure France that the Jay Treaty was not an anti-French treaty. Monroe was a peculiar choice for such a mission, because he himself had strongly opposed the treaty and had even accused Jay of accepting a bribe for signing it. A fervid admirer of France as well as a man who had called Britain "the enemy of mankind," Monroe did all he could while ambassador to undermine the administration's foreign policy. Moreover, he corresponded more frequently with fellow Republicans than with the State Department, and he wrote propaganda for Republican newspapers. In 1796, Washington finally recalled him, but the French, believing Monroe reflected the views of most Americans, were certain that if they interfered in American affairs they could rout the Federalists.

In 1796, the French were right in their assessment of American public opinion, though pro-French sentiment was perhaps not as strong as it had been in 1793 and 1794. Yet, the more they interfered in American politics, the more public opinion turned against them, so that by 1797 most Americans were anti-French and many even clamored for war with France. There were good reasons for the growing resentment of the French, resentment that finally turned into hatred. After Washington signed the Jay Treaty, the French attempted to defeat its implementation; the French minister undertook to direct Republican strategy in Congress by conferring with party leaders. Then France tried to influence the outcome of the presidential elections; in a series of newspaper articles, the French minister urged Americans to vote for Jefferson. If they did so, he said, they would restore themselves to the good graces of the French Republic; if they did not, then France would take a tougher line on the question of neutral shipping. When John Adams was elected, the French backed their threats with actions; they attacked American ships and confiscated the cargo as well as the vessels. France also dismissed the newly appointed American ambassador, saying that it would not receive another until its grievances had been redressed. As a result, the United States in 1797 found itself in a quasi war with France. Public opinion was no longer on the side of France. There were other reasons for the change in public opinion: France was no longer a republic but a country run by an oligarchy called the Directory; France had attacked and overthrown other republics, such as Switzerland and Holland; and finally, more and more books about the excesses of the French Revolution were being published in the United States. It became difficult for Americans to see any resemblance between the French Revolution and their own.

The last straw was the XYZ affair. In brief, three American envoys sent by Adams to negotiate differences with France in order to prevent a war were told by agents in the French ministry (designated in Adams's report to Congress as XYZ) that negotiations could take place only if they paid a bribe of $250,000 to Talleyrand and the Directory, advanced the government a loan of $12 million, and offered suitable apologies for the harsh remarks against France by President Adams in his message to Congress of 15 May 1797. In April 1798, the dispatches of the envoys regarding the matter were published and "electrified the country as had no other event since the Revolutionary War."[25] Now it was France that was corrupt—more corrupt than Britain, because the British had never conducted foreign policy in this manner. No longer was the United States racked by discord over foreign policy: Most Americans—Republican or Federalist, northern or southern—were anti-French. War with France was narrowly averted only because in 1798 English victories over the French fleet made France more willing to negotiate with the United States.

Riding the wave of anti-French sentiment, the Federalists became the dominant party in 1798 and 1799, only to lose their popularity with an astonishing quickness. "Compare the situation of the Federalists in 1798 with their present situation," a writer said in 1801, "and we find a party can never be too high, to fall."[26] Although there was no longer any question of French influence in the American government, the Federalists continued to believe Republicans were traitorous Jacobin conspirators. By contrast, the Republicans were more inclined to dismiss the question of foreign influence, especially because they had become disenchanted with France and had less reason to declaim against British iniquities. The Jay Treaty had been a success, bolstering the American economy, and the revolutionary war was becoming a dim memory. The nature of the two parties had changed: During the early years of the decade, the Republicans had been the party most governed by opinion—by their enthusiasm for the French Revolution; by the end of the decade, the Federalists became the party most governed by opinion—by their conviction that Republicans were the servile minions of France.

The threat of war with France had made Federalists more vituperative than ever. In 1797 Noah Webster, a Federalist who had previously shown some sympathy for the Republican position on the Jay Treaty, called the Republican opposition a "pack of scoundrels."[27] Such views persisted even when the threat of war with France had been removed. "Can serious and reflecting men look about them and doubt," the writer of a Federalist pamphlet for the elections of 1800 wondered, "that if Jefferson is elected, and the Jacobins get into authority, that those morals which protect our lives from the knife of the assassin . . . will not be trampled upon and exploded?"[28] Of course, because each party regarded the other as illegitimate, charges of treachery and corruption were commonplace, but Federalists were more disposed to act on their convictions. They not only castigated the Republicans, they also hounded them—trying to stifle dissent. In 1798 a Federalist majority in Congress assured passage of the Alien and Sedition Acts, a series of laws that precipitated what Richard Hofstadter calls "the most decisive crisis of the early Union."[29]

Of the three acts, the Act for the Punishment of Certain Crimes— popularly known as the Sedition Act—was the most important. It was clearly designed to emasculate the Republican opposition, for there was no real threat of sedition in the United States. Under the terms of the act, which were vague enough to make a man criminally liable for almost any criticism of the government, fifteen persons were indicted and eleven convicted. All were active Republicans. The Federalists' actions called forth a Republican response: In the fall of 1798, Jefferson drafted the Kentucky Resolution. Declaring the Union a compact between the states and the general government, Jefferson said that because the states are "sovereign and independent," they have the "unquestionable right" to judge whether a particular act of the general government is constitutional—and the right, moreover, to nullify those acts they deem unconstitutional. The Virginia Resolution, which was drafted by Madison a few month later, came to a more tempered conclusion, but it too assigned sovereignty to the states. A state legislature, Madison argued, has the right and duty both to interpose its authority when it deems certain federal laws unconstitutional and to call upon sister states in securing their repeal.

The Virginia and Kentucky Resolutions signified a defiance of federal authority. And defiance, if not outright secession, was in the air in 1799. Some Virginians spoke of the federal government "as an enemy infinitely more formidable and infinitely more to be guarded against than the French Directory,"[30] and there were reports of military preparations in the state, the arming of the militia and the construction of an armory in Richmond. If, on the strength of the reports, the federal government had decided to send in troops, Virginians may have met force with force. Hamilton, knowing full well what might happen, nevertheless advocated such a policy because he was eager to see the state divided into more manageable jurisdictions. But his views did not prevail. By 1799, in fact, they rarely prevailed, because President Adams had become increasingly distrustful of the advice he was getting from the Hamiltonian wing of the party. In 1799, contrary to the wishes of Hamilton and his followers, Adams sent three envoys to Paris to negotiate a treaty with a French government that, because it was preoccupied with fighting the Second Coalition, was eager to come to terms with the United States. With the threat of war removed, Federalists could not muster enough support to renew the Alien and Sedition Acts, and the Sedition Act itself expired on 3 March 1801, the day before Jefferson's inauguration, an inauguration that saw the peaceful transfer of power to an opposition party that had been regarded as illegitimate and subversive. The crisis of the Union had been weathered.

The seriousness of the crisis, however, should not be underestimated. Taken literally, the Virginia and Kentucky Resolutions were a giant step in the direction of undermining the Union. The Alien and Sedition Acts called for a strong response, but many Republicans thought the resolutions went too far, and a considerable minority of the Virginia legislature opposed them. Madison's argument is perplexing. The position he took, according to Richard B. Morris, "seems extraordinarily paradoxical and completely inconsistent with his previously held constitutional views. . . ."[31] As a practical politician, however, Madison preferred expediency to consistency, and he may have felt that only such a strongly worded resolution could have headed off actual defiance on the part of many southerners. Jefferson himself, after first hearing of the laws, had suggested that the states announce their intention of seceding from the Union should the laws remain in force.

On his deathbed many years later, when the doctrines of nullification and secession were on the rise, Madison felt the need to say that he no longer supported notions of states' rights that might undermine the Union: "The advice nearest to my heart and deepest in my convictions is that the Union of the States be cherished and perpetuated."[32] Despite the strong words of the Virginia Resolution, Madison had no desire to provoke a crisis of the Union, and Jefferson soon came round to his opinion. "We should never think of separation but for repeated and enormous violations," Jefferson said, and he counseled his more radical followers against violence: "This is not the kind of opposition the American people will permit. But keep away all show of force, and they will bear down the evil propensities of the government by the constitutional means of election & petition."[33]

When Jefferson speaks of "what the American people will permit," he is revealing his faith in the self-correcting nature of republican government. In the long run, he implies, "the evil propensities of government" will be contained by constitutional means. Republicans had faith in the ability of republican government to take care of itself, as it were, whereas Federalists did not. The Federalists thought republican government a frail creature that could not survive if it did not accept their ministrations. Regarding themselves as a governing elite, the Federalists put little trust in the average American's ability to discern what was in the public interest, and were fearful that if their prescriptions were not followed things would fall apart. In 1792, Hamilton had confided to a friend that he was "affectionately attached to the republican theory" but that he considered "its success as yet a problem. It is yet to be determined by experience whether it be consistent with that stability and order in government which are essential to public strength and private security and happiness."[34] By the end of the decade Hamilton's confidence—and the confidence of most Federalists—had eroded. And in 1802, a disillusioned Hamilton could write to a friend: "Perhaps no man in the United States has sacrificed or done more for the present Constitution than myself; and contrary to all my anticipations of its fate, as you know from the very beginning, I am still laboring to prop the frail and worthless fabric."[35]

In the late 1790s, not every Federalist thought the Constitution was a "worthless fabric," but many were certain that only they possessed the wisdom and virtue to govern. The Federalists expected deference, yet as citizens loyal to a republican form of government, they realized that they had to court public opinion if they wanted to remain in power. "The first thing in all great operations of such a government as ours," Hamilton said, "is to secure the opinion of the people."[36] The Federalists knew that they could not simply instruct the public in "salutary truths," as one Federalist put it; they had to persuade the public that the salutary truths were valid.

It was easier, however, for the Federalists to acknowledge the need for persuasion than to be actually persuasive. They found it difficult to do anything but talk down to the public, to admit that public opinion was ever in the right. As the decade progressed, many Federalists began to take satisfaction in being unpopular, as if that were a sign of the correctness of their views. To try to secure the opinion of the people would be demeaning. Only Republicans, they thought, could stoop so low, and that is why the Republican party had won a sweeping victory in 1800, gaining majorities in both the House and the Senate and making strong inroads in such traditionally Federalist strongholds as New York and Massachusetts.

Federalist postmortems harped on the point that the Republicans had won so handily because they knew how to appeal to the people—knew, that is, how to stoop. In competition with their Republican opponents, the Federalists, in the characterization of Fisher Ames, were like "flat tranquility against passion; dry leaves against the whirlwind; the weight of gunpowder against its kindled force."[37] Hamilton makes much the same point: "Men are rather reasoning than reasonable animals, for the most part governed by the impulse of passion. This is a truth well understood by our adversaries, who have practised upon it with no small benefit to their cause. . . ." The Federalists, he concludes, "erred in relying so much on the rectitude and utility of their measures as to have neglected the cultivation of popular favor, by fair and justifiable expedients."[38] In short, as Noah Webster says, the Federalists had "manifested more integrity than address."[39] They had thought reason would prevail, but it was clear that elections were won not by being reasonable but by appealing to the passions.

No doubt, these postmortems consoled the Federalists, reassuring them that their political failures were the result of their personal dignity and integrity. But the postmortems were not an accurate diagnosis of the party's collapse. The party did poorly in the election of 1800 *not* because it was composed of reasonable men who had refrained from appealing to the passions. It did poorly because Federalists were regarded as far too passionate and unreasoning. Many Americans thought them obsessed with the dangers of Jacobinism—obsessed with conspiracy when there was no evidence to give credence to their fears.

In 1797, "conspiracy" was a word very much bandied about by prominent Federalists. Since the beginning of the decade, Federalists had been disposed to regard Republicans as would-be Jacobins, but in 1787 a notorious book about the Bavarian Illuminati had turned those suspicions into vehement convictions. An anticlerical European society that espoused the principles of the Enlightenment and numbered among its members several distinguished writers, the Bavarian Illuminati was little more than an exotic name to Federalists until John Robison, a well-known Scottish scientist, published a book that claimed the Illuminati was formed "for the express purpose of ROOTING OUT ALL THE RELIGIOUS ESTABLISH-MENTS AND OVERTURNING ALL THE EXISTING GOVERN-MENTS of Europe."[40] Robison argued, moreover, that the Illumnati had played a major role in bringing about the French Revolution and that most of the active leaders of the Revolution belonged to the society.

The effect of Robison's book on many Federalists was dramatic. In 1795 Jedidiah Morse, a leading Bostonian clergyman and a geographer of international reputation, had lavishly praised Robespierre and had given the French Revolution a higher rating than the American Revolution. Then in May of 1798, after having read Robison's book, he became violently anti-French, convinced that the United States was in grave danger of being undermined by a Jacobinical plot touched off by the Illuminati. Because of Morse's prominence as well as the prominence of other Federalists who agreed with him, talk of conspiracy became commonplace among Federalists, and this sentiment surely contributed to the passage of the Alien and Sedition Acts.

It is easy to see why in 1798, when the United States was engaged in a quasi war with France, talk of conspiracy became commonplace. But even in 1800 many Federalists continued to ride the same hobbyhorse. It is doubtful that they made much of conspiracy because they truly believed there was a vast number of Illuminati trying to subvert the American government. Rather, it was their fear of domestic faction that made them dwell so much on conspiracy. Conspiracy thrives, they said, in an atmosphere of factional discord. Eliminate faction and conspiracy would wither away. So, at least, reasoned Robert Goodlow Harper, a prominent Federalist, during the congressional debates over the Alien and Sedition bills. Recent events in Europe, Harper maintained, proved how "republican governments are especially menaced with destruction [by] the introduction of foreign influence"—a foreign influence that "supports, and is supported by, domestic faction."[41] According to most Federalists, republican government was a frail creature that could withstand being infected by foreign influence only if it lived in a salubrious climate—one, that is, without faction.

In holding these beliefs, the Federalists were conforming to the tenets of classical political theory about the nature of republics, but they were repudiating the revised republican theory of Publius, the theory that provided the basis for an extended commercial republic. The public interest, they were certain, could be determined only by men like themselves, whose business it was to "rectify" popular errors and castigate "popular delusions." Publius thought the representatives of the people should "refine and enlarge" upon public opinion; the Federalists preferred to scorn public opinion altogether.

The Republicans were more willing to listen to public opinion. When, in his message to Congress in 1794, Washington had denounced the Democrat Societies (political clubs loosely modeled on those that had been formed in France after the Revolution) as "prime movers of the Whiskey Rebellion," Madison responded that censoring such clubs would be unconstitutional. The right of discussing, writing, and publishing, he said, could not legally be invaded by the federal government. "The censorial power is in the people over the Government, and not in the Government over the people."[42] He made much the same point four years later when he said in the Virginia Resolution that the Sedition Act was "a power which more than any other ought to produce universal alarm, because it is levelled against the right of freely examining public characters and measures. . . ."[43] As the opposition party, the Republicans had no choice but to argue against such governmental measures, but even after 1800, when their party was in power, they remained firmly committed to the unlimited circulation of opinion. In his inaugural address, Jefferson held that opinions about government and governors were many and diverse, and that all political opinions ought to be allowed to "stand undisturbed as monuments of the safety with which error of opinion may be tolerated where reason is left free to combat it."[44] Only if all opinions were allowed to be heard could deliberation truly take place and some notion of what was in the public interest emerge. The Federalists disagreed: The flowering of opinions would enable noxious opinions to flourish; the bad opinions would drive out the good; and the result would be subversion, then anarchy, and finally despotism.

Preoccupied with stamping out dissent and ferreting out conspiracy, the Federalists sounded very much like the patriots of old. They justified the extreme measures called for in the Alien and Sedition Acts by arguing that the forces threatening the United States in 1798 were similar to those Americans had faced during the Revolution. Instead of a corrupt monarchy, they were now struggling against an international Jacobin conspiracy —a struggle more difficult because the enemy was conspiratorial. The enemy did not attack in the open; it secretly worked away at public opinion by making sure the press was on its side. Bent on prosecuting the Republican press, Federalists said that "libels" by "corrupt partisans and hired presses" had enabled France to sap the will of many European nations to resist it.[45] The same tactics, the Federalists claimed, were being used in the United States. France was the new Old-World tyrant, spreading its own brand of corruption: not the corruption of private interests and economic privilege but the "corruption" that goes with democracy, atheism, and anarchy. Stirred by their fears of this new tyrant, Samuel Adams and Patrick Henry—two old firebrand patriots—allied themselves with the Federalists.

Hating the French Revolution and fearful of an international Jacobin conspiracy, the Federalists misread the public temper in ways that led to their downfall. "Their crime," alleges Louis Hartz, "was not villainy but stupidity. . . ."[46] Their crime, we might add, was that they were men of little faith in the American form of representative government—little faith, moreover, in the circulation of opinion. They believed that Americans should defer to them as men who knew what was best for the country, but Americans were not in the habit of deferring to anyone.

The workings of American politics in the 1790s, then, were different from what Madison and Hamilton had envisioned. In the first place, there was not a "multiplicity of interests" but two broad regional interests—the agricultural South and the commercial North. More important, parties from principle arose—parties that were more inclined to vex and oppress each other than to cooperate for the common good. In such a political climate, where a "zeal for different opinions" flourished, it was exceedingly difficult to regulate "various and interfering interests."

By the end of the decade, however, only the Federalist party was truly a party from principle, and the Federalist party faded fast. By the 1820s, as Hofstadter says, a second generation of political leaders arose who were "considerably more interested than their predecessors in organization, considerably less fixed in their view of issues, considerably less ideological."[47] In short, they were modern political professionals who cared less about ideas than about organizational discipline, and the parties they founded were clusters of special interests bound together by only a vague allegiance to a loose set of ideas. Writing in 1844, Emerson acknowledges this state of affairs, and implies approval. "Ordinarily," he says in "Politics," "our parties are parties from circumstance, and not of principle; as the planting interest in conflict with the commercial, . . . parties which are identical in their moral character, and which can easily change ground with each other in the support of many of their measures. Parties of principle, as, religious sects, or the party of free-trade, of universal suffrage, of abolition of slavery, of abolition of capital punishment, degenerate into personalities, or would inspire enthusiasm."[48] And it was the main function of party professionals to make sure that parties from interest—or Emerson's "parties from circumstance"—did not become so infected with opinion that they became parties from principle. As Seymour Martin Lipset says, "The American propensity to moralistic and extreme politics has been effectively countered by the compromise coalition politics characteristic of our party system."[49]

Thus, the rise of a two-party system, something Publius had not foreseen, has been a boon to Publius's science of politics, for it is doubtful that "various and interfering interests" could be regulated without such a system. The system, of course, has not been wholly effective. As we know, parties from principle did not disappear after the 1790s; they flourished in the 1840s and 1850s, leading to the Civil War. Moreover, after the Civil War, Publius's science of politics was threatened for a completely different reason: corruption. According to many contemporary observers, the republican form of government of the United States was in dire straits because politicians no longer regulated various and interfering interests; they simply did their bidding. If politicians were bribed by the special interests, then Publius's science of politics was a failure, for legislators were no longer pursuing "great and national objects." But was the assessment of those who attacked political corruption right?

Notes

1. Cited, John C. Miller, *The Federalist Era: 1789–1801* (New York: Harper & Row, 1960), p. 51.
2. Ibid., p. 47.
3. Ibid., p. 41.
4. Ibid., p. 51.
5. Cited, Felix Gilbert, *The Beginnings of American Foreign Policy* (New York: Harper & Row, 1965), p. 131.
6. Clinton Rossiter, ed., *The Federalist Papers* (New York: New American Library, 1961), pp. 160; 91; 256.
7. Richard Buel, Jr., *Securing the Revolution: Ideology in American Politics, 1789–1815* (Ithaca: Cornell University Press, 1972), p. 74.
8. Noble E. Cunningham, Jr., cited, Richard Hofstadter, *The Idea of a Party System* (Berkeley: University of California Press, 1970), p. 88.
9. Cited, Marvin Meyers, ed., *The Mind of the Founder* (Indianapolis: Bobbs-Merrill, 1973), pp. 240–41.
10. Cited, *The Philosophy of Edmund Burke,* ed. Louis I. Bredvold and Ralph G. Ross (Ann Arbor: University of Michigan Press, 1967), p. 35.
11. Noble E. Cunningham, Jr., ed., *The Making of the American Party System* (Englewood Cliffs, N.J.: Prentice-Hall, 1965), p. 11.
12. Ibid.
13. Ibid., p. 41.
14. Ibid.
15. Cited, Miller, *Federalist Era,* p. 81.
16. Cunningham, *Making of the American Party System,* p. 40.
17. Cited, Hofstadter, *Idea of a Party System,* p. 89.
18. Cited, R. R. Palmer, *The World of the French Revolution* (New York: Harper & Row, 1971), p. 226.
19. Ibid.
20. Cited, John C. Miller, *Alexander Hamilton and the Growth of the New Nation* (New York: Harper & Row, 1964), p. 369.
21. Cited, Buel, *Securing the Revolution,* p. 47.

22. Ibid., p. 66.
23. Hofstadter, *Idea of a Party System,* p. 90.
24. Cited, Miller, *Federalist Era,* p. 164.
25. Ibid., p. 212.
26. Ibid., p. 274.
27. Cited, Miller, *Federalist Era,* p. 233.
28. Cunningham, *Making of the American Party System,* p. 152.
29. Hofstadter, *Idea of a Party System,* p. 102.
30. Cited, Miller, *Federalist Era,* p. 237.
31. Richard B. Morris, *Seven Who Shaped Our Destiny: The Founding Fathers as Revolutionaries* (New York: Harper & Row, 1973), p. 219.
32. Meyers, *Mind of the Founder,* p. 576.
33. Cited, Miller, *Federalist Era,* p. 242.
34. *The Basic Ideas of Alexander Hamilton,* ed. Richard B. Morris (New York: Pocket Books, 1957), pp. 96–97.
35. Ibid., p. 440.
36. Cited, Gordon S. Wood, "The Democratization of Mind in the American Revolution," in *The Moral Foundations of the American Republic,* ed. Robert H. Horwitz (Charlottesville: University Press of Virginia, 1977), p. 120.
37. Ibid.
38. Cited, Gerald Stourzh, *Alexander Hamilton and the Idea of Republican Government* (Stanford: Stanford University Press, 1970), p. 123.
39. Cited, Miller, *Federalist Era,* p. 276.
40. Cited, Richard Hofstadter, *The Paranoid Style in American Politics* (New York: Alfred A. Knopf, 1964), p. 11.
41. Cited, Buel, *Securing the Revolution,* pp. 194–95.
42. Cited, Miller, *Federalist Era,* pp. 160, 162.
43. Cited, Hofstadter, p. 113.
44. Richard Hofstadter, ed., *Great Issues in American History: From the Revolution to the Civil War, 1765–1865* (New York: Random House, 1958), p. 188.
45. See Buel, *Securing the Revolution,* p. 247.
46. Louis Hartz, *The Liberal Tradition in America* (New York: Harcourt, Brace & World, 1955), p. 95.
47. Hofstadter, *Idea of a Party System,* p. 213.
48. *Emerson: Selected Prose and Poetry,* ed. Reginald W. Cook (New York: Rinehart, 1955), p. 199.
49. Seymour Martin Lipset, "The Paradox of American Politics," in *The American Commonwealth: 1976* (New York: Basic Books, 1976), pp. 154–55.

5
The Gilded Age: Mugwumps versus the Machine

In 1874, approximately two generations after the Federalists had suffered defeat in the election of 1800, a group of distinguished New Englanders, including three of John Adams's grandchildren, met in Boston to discuss forming a "party of the center." By "center" they did not mean somewhere between the two parties. They were less a party than an independent force in politics, one that hoped to move the major parties in the direction of reform. Theirs was the politics of disinterested men, the politics of what they called "the best men."[1] The reformers, who came to be called Mugwumps, despised the politics of the Gilded Age. According to them, "professional politician" (or "machine politician") was a term of opprobrium, for professional politicians were venal and corrupt. As early as 1866, the *Nation,* the leading journal of reform opinion, declaimed that "the diminution of political corruption is the great question of our time."[2]

E. L. Godkin, the *Nation's* editor, was a leading voice of the reform movement, as were George W. Curtis, the editor of *Harper's Weekly,* and Henry Adams, who in the 1870s edited the *North American Review.* The reformers were "the best men" insofar as they were leading intellectuals, academics, journalists, and businessmen. They spoke, as they said, for the "educated classes," and to "the honest intelligent, industrious population of all grades,"[3] a category that did not include the new immigrants who thronged the streets of New York, Boston, and other eastern cities—immigrants who, the reformers claimed, were easily manipulated by unscrupulous professional politicians.

For several reasons, the reformers never became a strong force in American politics. The "party of the center" carried no important elections, and placed few representatives in office. The reformers were ineffectual in part because they found it difficult to act in unison. Proud of their independent views, they often quarreled among themselves. They were also ineffectual because they could not divest themselves of their basic contempt for politics.

Expecting their views to prevail because of the deference owed to members of the "educated classes," they quickly became disillusioned when those whom they despised—the professional politicians—did not rush to agree with them. Two years after Adams had urged the formation of a party of the center, he complained that "politics have ceased to interest me."[4] According to Adams, corruption was so rife that reformers would be condemning themselves to "a life of wasted energy" if they attempted to sweep Washington politics "clean of the endless corruption. . . ."[5]

The reformers' disdain for professional politicians made them disagreeable even to politicians who were sympathetic to many of their causes. Needless to say, politicians who opposed their reforms usually returned scorn for scorn. Senator Roscoe Conkling accused the reformers of hypocrisy: "Their vocation and ministry is to lament the sins of other people. Their stock in trade is rancid, canting self-righteousness. They are wolves in sheep's clothing. Their real object is office and plunder. When Dr. Johnson defined patriotism as the last refuge of a scoundrel, he was unconscious of the then undeveloped capabilities and uses of the word 'Reform'."[6] But the reformers were not scoundrels, and "reform" was not simply a means to power, although they certainly were animated by the desire to see "the best men" in positions of leadership. Rather, the reformers were men of little faith in the political process. Assuming that men who held views different from their own were corrupt or—at the very least—narrowly self-interested, the reformers found it difficult to engage in the act of persuasion. They believed that they alone were right about matters of public policy because they alone were disinterested, public-spirited men.

Recalling the Gilded Age in his autobiography, written some forty years later, Henry Adams says: "The political dilemma was as clear in 1870 as it was likely to be in 1970. The system of 1789 had broken down, . . ."[7] Adams's "system of 1789," however, bears little resemblance to what Publius thought the system should be. According to Adams, it was "a system of a priori, or moral, principles." Moreover, what he laments as dismal fact seems remarkably like what Publius had intended. "Nine-tenths of men's political energies," Adams says, "must henceforth be wasted on expedients to piece out—to patch—or, in vulgar language, to tinker—the political machine as often as it broke down."[8] Tinkering was, in part, what Publius had in mind. But what if, as the reformers claimed, politicians did not simply try to seek accommodation among interests but sold their votes on issues to the highest bidder? What if congressmen not only listened to different interests but were actually beholden to some of them for favors, financial or otherwise? If such was the case, then the system of 1789 had indeed broken down; enlightened self-interest was not at work but only unscrupulous private interest.

Was American politics during the Gilded Age truly an Augean stable? The number of scandals unearthed during the 1870s (the Tweed Ring, Credit Mobilier, the Whiskey Ring, and the Indian Agency Ring) led many to believe that legislative bribery with corporate money was rampant. Writing in 1870 about the financial skulduggery of the Erie Railway, Henry Adams complained that it had "proved itself able to override and trample on law, custom, decency, and every restraint known to society, without scruple, and as yet without check." Its activities were a warning that the corporation—the new breed of business arrangement that began to flourish after the Civil War—"is in its nature a threat against the popular institutions spreading so rapidly over the whole world."9 The corporation, he suggested, was a threat to representative government.

There is no question that many corporations tried to influence the course of legislation by whatever means they could. And there can be no doubt that in a few states a corporation dominated the legislature so completely that it had a strong say in selecting senators. According to one reformer, Standard Oil did everything to the Pennsylvania legislature except refine it; and in 1869 a Harrisburg newspaper estimated that only 22 out of 133 Pennsylvania legislators were honest. In local politics, officeholder and contractor kickbacks were established facts. Moreover, voting practices—especially in the big cities—were corrupt: Ballots were peddled, going for as much as fifty dollars, and voters were imported from other districts or states. These and other irregularities apparently were pervasive, but the advantages gained by a particular party were not necessarily advantages that accrued to corporations. By establishing their own political fiefdoms, city bosses could resist the bribes or threats of corporations.

In Washington, bribery was certainly less commonplace than in state and local politics, but even there swarming lobbyists attempted to influence the legislative process. One favored tactic was deliberately to lose to legislators at cards. Corruption existed, but determining its extent is not easy. Henry Adams placed the number of openly corrupt congressmen at 10 percent, but virtually all historians of the period find the estimate excessive. Indeed, some historians have concluded that the lurid reports of journalists and reformers are in the main works of fiction. "Political careers," David Rothman states, "demanded too much time and energy for anyone primarily dedicated to furthering financial enterprises."10 People went into politics because they were interested in politics, not because they wanted to become rich. Being a senator was a financial hardship, which is perhaps why the prevailing attitude toward conflicts of interest was more lenient then than today. Adams notwithstanding, during the Gilded Age the crooked politician was by far the exception rather than the rule.

But even if Adams is right and many congressmen were hogs rooting in an Augean stable, it does not necessarily follow that corruption significantly affected the legislative process. Corporations did not dictate political decisions because, among other things, their efforts often were at cross purposes. There was no uniform business interest. Railroad regulatory legislation was favored by some businessmen, opposed by others; some manufacturers preferred high tariffs, others did not; and some capitalists urged inflationary measures while others advocated currency contraction. Legislators were importuned by a wide range of lobbyists from the business world, each with a list of desired measures. Even if a legislator accepted favors from a corporation—if not outright bribery, then stock options or jobs for relatives —he usually felt that he was obliged only to hear its arguments, not invariably to support its position. Politics was an intricate activity, and the legislator had other interests to assuage, other requests to meet. Some corporations spent a good deal of time and money trying to influence the legislative process, but the results were often not what they desired.

Corporations were also frustrated because of the weakness of party organization in the 1870s and 1880s. Congressmen were less members of a party than adherents of particular factions—Stalwarts, Half-Breeds, Bourbons, anti-Bourbons—and it was difficult for a congressional leader to command enough support to get a bill passed. The fate of legislation usually rested with a large, diverse body of legislators, and the voting behavior of many was erratic and unpredictable. Faced with such congressional disorder, corporations found it difficult to use their money wisely. Some corporations hedged their bets, contributing to the campaigns of all the candidates; others abandoned expensive lobbying efforts. "Despite significant expenditures and efforts, from the most legitimate to the most questionable, business interests could not efficiently prejudice the legislative process."[11] The rise of the corporation proved less of a threat to politics than Adams had thought. In deliberating upon matters of public policy, most congressmen had to accommodate "a multiplicity of interests," not only the interests of the corporate world.

To call the Congress a deliberative body, however, may be a misnomer. During the 1870s and 1880s, the House of Representatives was, according to Woodrow Wilson, "a disintegrate mass of jarring elements."[12] It was governed by a mass of archaic rules that were calculated, as one of its members said, "to disturb legislators and obstruct legislation." The procedural chaos was compounded by the ill-mannered conduct of legislators who seldom paid full attention to the matters at hand. "House discussion," one congressman complained, "had little deliberation in it," and another remarked that "the House is losing its freedom of debate, of amendment, even of knowledge." The result was stasis: Few significant bills were passed in the House, which was often criticized in the press for "slowly doing nothing."[13] The Senate's proceedings were far more decorous and measures were debated more fully, yet even the Senate was unproductive.

The politics of the Gilded Age appears so "remarkably vacuous and fruitless,"[14] as John Garraty remarks, because legislators had no clear sense of how to respond to the new industrial order that had arisen since the Civil War. And they received no direction on matters of public policy from the electorate, for presidential as well as congressional elections revealed no clear drift in public opinion. In 1872, Grant won by a landslide, perhaps because his opponent was widely regarded as incompetent, but the next four presidential elections were extremely close. In two of them—the election of 1876 and the election of 1888—the man who became president did not win a plurality of the popular vote. Hayes, Garfield, Cleveland, and Harrison all squeaked into office, lacking a strong mandate; and Chester Arthur, who became president after Garfield's assassination, had no mandate from anybody. These presidents may not have been men of vision and imagination, but even if they had been more dynamic leaders they would not have been able to accomplish much, for rarely in the Gilded Age did a president have the full support of his party.

The prevalence of party factions made it difficult to know where legislators stood. The parties differed, of course, on the major issues of the day, but in the welter of factional disputes their positions were often abandoned. Moreover, the nature of the issues was such that legislators were especially given to equivocation. Tariff policy and monetary policy—two of the major issues—did not readily lend themselves to clarification, and legislators found it difficult to know what might benefit their constituents as well as the country in general.

The tariff question did not so much as divide public opinion as fracture it into innumerable fragments, fragments that did not easily align themselves by party. Because most Americans were for tariffs—only doctrinaire Social Darwinists and classical economists opposed them altogether—congressional debate centered on the appropriate level of duties and on which foreign manufactures should be taxed. Tariff policy was surely something that only a few Americans agonized over, but among them were reformers, who were disturbed that the current level of duties enabled the Treasury to take in more money than it spent, and legislators from districts whose industries were vulnerable to an influx of cheap foreign goods. Shortly after Grover Cleveland was elected president, he confessed to a prominent reformer, "The truth is I know nothing about the tariff. . . . Will you tell me how to go about it to learn?"[15] According to one report, he leaned forward wearily as he said this. Most congressmen probably faced the tariff question with the same degree of enthusiasm.

Monetary policy, on the other hand, engaged the passions as no other

issue did during the Gilded Age. It was a subject that bred misunderstand-
ing and confusion. As a bewildered constituent complained to his senator
in 1878: "In the great diversity of opinion existing amongst minds equally
educated, it is difficult to know where the *right* is." The "right" was clear
to those who supported a so-called natural monetary system, one based
upon a fixed, immutable gold standard. The *New York Christian Advocate*
railed against the greenbackers—those who supported a paper currency
backed only by the credit of the United States and not convertible into gold
or silver—in 1878: "Atheism is not worse in religion than an unstable or
irredeemable currency in political economy."[16] Taking a position similar to
the *Advocate*'s, the Republican party supported "sound money," whereas
the Democratic party supported monetary expansion. But the politics of the
money question is extremely complicated and party alignments are of little
help in determining where a congressman stood on the question. The financial legislation that eventuated took the form of compromises that were
satisfactory to no one; several times acts were passed, only to be repealed
a few years later. It was not until the turn of the century that the issue lost
its sting, probably to the relief of many legislators. Some of them may have
remembered Garfield's remark about a certain congressman, David Meilish
of New York: "He devoted himself almost exclusively to the study of the
currency, became fully entangled with the theories of the subject and
became insane."[17]

Insanity, of course, was not the usual reward for devotion to the money
question. Legislators were not unsettled by it but disturbed about it—and
disturbed, in general, that the realities of the postwar economy had outpaced orthodox theories of political economy. Legislators had little in the
way of economic information, legal knowledge, and historic precedent to
rely on as guides to coping with the new industrial order. Many people
worried about the power of the corporation, and during the 1870s some
candidates rode into office by attacking the railroads, but many people were
also aware that the rise of the corporation had resulted in increased produc-
tivity, creating jobs and wealth. How to control corporate power without
hurting corporate efficiency was a question on the minds of many legislators
as they addressed the major issues of the day. Most congressmen were not
corrupt; they were in the main thoughtful men who were groping toward
legislation that might shape economic growth without stifling it. The *Congressional Record* for the years 1877–1896, one historian argues, bears
comparison with that of any other generation, revealing a responsible group
of leaders—whatever their differences.[18]

The professional politician was not as dishonest as the reformers made
him out to be. But, more important, the professional politician was, in
general, more willing than the reformers to entertain new ideas about the

relation of government to the economy. What most moderate and responsible politicians thought about the new order can perhaps be gleaned from an entry Rutherford Hayes made in his diary after having reluctantly authorized federal troops to quell the railroad strike of 1877. "The strikes have been put down by *force,* but now for the real remedy. Can't something be done by education of the strikers, *by judicious control of the capitalists,* by wise general policy to end or diminish the evil? The railroad strikers, as a rule, are good men, sober, intelligent, and industrious" (emphasis added). Hayes did not consider capitalism a "natural" force that could not be tampered with, but he did not know what kind of legislation would promote "judicious control of the capitalists."[19] As he noted in his diary in 1878: "We are in a period when old questions are settled, and the new ones are not yet brought forward. Extreme party action, if continued in such a time, would ruin the [Republican] party. Moderation is its only chance."[20] Like most legislators, Hayes thought the times required prudence and forbearance; the times also required a certain willingness to entertain new ideas.

Charles Francis Adams, a founding member of the "party of the center," was not disposed to entertain new ideas about the postwar polity. Unlike Hayes, he was certain about what government should do: It should make the new industrial order conform to the "natural" laws of economics, which meant that the government should refrain from regulating as well as subventing railroads. "Competition will regulate where it has free, full play," Adams explained, "but where it has not such full, clear play, it must confound."[21] Adams testified before Congress that the "law of competition" would correct railroad abuse. The "law of competition" also meant that unions should not be tolerated, because they prevented free competition for wages and profits. The railroad strike of 1877 prompted Adams to comment, "The Brotherhood of Locomotive Engineers has got to be broken up. It has become . . . a standing public menace."[22] More than most politicians, the reformers resisted the notion that the doctrine of laissez faire was no longer an adequate explanation of economic reality. The evils of the new industrial order, they argued, had come about because laissez faire had not been scrupulously adhered to.

The reformers may have been defenders of laissez faire, but they were not apologists for big business. The reformers scorned the plutocrats as immoral and irresponsible men who, in their obsession with making money, sought special privileges from the government. Although some plutocrats, when they wanted to thwart government regulations, found themselves citing the wisdom of the reformers, many were uneasy about aligning themselves with men in thrall to ideas gleaned from classic texts of economic theory as well as from professors of economics, for until the mid-1880s laissez faire remained unquestioned in the university. The reformers saw themselves as defenders of liberal individualism, defenders of a free enterprise untainted by government intervention. They favored "sound money" because they thought the government should not regulate the money supply by issuing irredeemable currency, and they favored free trade because they thought tariffs flouted the "law of supply and demand" by interfering with the free play of wages and prices. In many ways, then, the reformers were not hospitable to reform.

No reformer was a more vociferous and passionate exponent of laissez faire than E. L. Godkin. The pages of the *Nation* were filled with his scathing attacks on those who went against orthodox economic theory. An Irishman who had imbibed his political economy in Ireland and England, he considered himself a disciple of Mill, though Mill—and most English liberals—were no longer steadfast opponents of all governmental intervention in the marketplace. Godkin, like Charles Adams, disapproved of attempts to regulate railroad rates, but he was characteristically more vehement than Adams, saying that all such attempts were "spoliation as flagrant as any proposed by Karl Marx." Godkin was convinced that if what he called the "real science" of political economy—a science consisting simply of "the knowledge of what man, as an exchanging, producing animal, would do, if let alone"—was not obeyed, the American polity would be undermined and eventually collapse. The best instructions any legislature could receive from the people would be "let us alone."[23]

Godkin, like Adams, did not support big business. Indeed, he may have been responsible for the phrase "robber baron," for in 1869 he called Cornelius Vanderbilt of the New York Central Railroad "a lineal successor of the medieval baron that we read about who . . . had the heart and hand to levy contributions on all who passed his way."[24] Godkin disapproved of the new plutocrats because they often disregarded the laws of political economy when they thought it in their interest to do so; they asked for special privileges from the government to prevent wages and prices from seeking their "natural" levels. Nevertheless, Godkin found himself more disposed to think well of businessmen than of what he called "labor agitators" and "communistic agrarians." The businessman, he thought, was basically a force for good, a force that was appointed by "natural selection" to invest capital to the best advantage of all Americans. Some businessmen, Godkin admitted, were guilty of abuses, but they were not threats to the system itself; unions were.[25]

Defending laissez faire, Godkin spoke of "natural laws"; and defending the hegemony of the businessman, he spoke of "natural selection." Like many reformers, he believed that his notions of political economy were "natural" in that they conformed to the laws of science. And, like many reformers, he was strengthened in his beliefs by the work of the English social philosopher Herbert Spencer, whose books sold extraordinarily well in the United States during the 1860s and 1870s. Although Spencer had published his most influential work some ten years before Darwin published *The Origin of Species* (1859), Spencer's work basked in the subsequent glow of Darwin's, for what Spencer said seemed to conform to the principles of evolutionary biology. "Under the natural order of things," Spencer argues, "society is constantly excreting its unhealthy, imbecile, slow, vacillating, faithless members" to leave more room for the deserving. Many Americans found sustenance in such an idea, because it meant that in pursuing one's self-interest one was obeying, in some mysterious way, God's plan, for Spencer claims that the miseries endured by the poor "are the decrees of a large, far-seeing benevolence"[26]—decrees that lead man onward and upward by preventing less fit human beings from flourishing.

Insofar as the reformers swallowed the principles of Spencer, they found themselves in the peculiar position of men who out of a disinterested patriotism advocated not the enlightened self-interest of Publius but the narrow self-interest of "natural selection." It was hard to do otherwise, because the latter was clothed in a scientific and even theological legitimacy. One commentator wrote in the *Atlantic Monthly* in 1882: The scientific party can only "defend the principle of competition, conformity to the law of supply and demand, and a fair field for the experiment of the survival of the fittest."[27] In Spencer, as in Mandeville, what appears to be bad—poverty and disease in Spencer, selfishness and luxury in Mandeville—works in the long run for the public good. But Spencer's justification of self-interest is a much more grandiose explanation of social and political life than Mandeville's modest and witty deflation of Bolingbroke's patriotism.

But too much should not be made of Spencer's Social Darwinism. For one thing, many Americans, including the reformers, were nourished on a Protestantism that stressed not only self-help but also compassion for the poor. Second, Godkin built his case for a self-regulating economy on classical liberalism, not Social Darwinism. The stock phrases of Social Darwinism rarely crop up in the writing of reformers. Perhaps the reformers remained wary of Social Darwinism because they realized that the laws of natural selection might be at odds with the laws of political economy—that natural selection, in fact, could be adduced as a justification for any conduct, including seeking special privileges from the government. The fittest, surely, were those who were cleverest at the game of survival.

Whatever we label the farrago of thought—imprecise notions gleaned from Adam Smith, John Stuart Mill, and Herbert Spencer—served up in the pages of the *Nation,* the *North American Review,* and *Harper's Weekly* during the two decades that followed the Civil War, it had a curious hold on many reformers. Social Darwinism made change the result of a quasi-mystical force called evolution; human action was unavailing. When asked what he would do about the political corruption of New York—a corruption that he had fervently denounced—a prominent Social Darwinist replied: "Nothing! You and I can do nothing at all. It's a matter of evolution. We can only wait for evolution. Perhaps in four or five thousand years evolution may have carried men beyond this state of things."[28] Most liberal reformers would have balked at carrying passivity to such extremes, but they also found it hard to act. The reformers' political philosophy was essentially quietist—and fatalistic: Man must rely on his own efforts; it was up to him whether he would rise or fall in the world. Concerted political action seemed beside the point, and even a betrayal of liberal principles. But the reformers were not alone in their faith in laissez faire. In the two decades that followed the Civil War, most Americans were governed by the opinion that the laws of political economy and the laws of natural selection required government to refrain from trying to shape the new industrial order, and that such a quietist policy was both scientifically correct and morally right.

The realities of the new industrial order, however, eventually undermined such opinions. "Competition," one railroad official said in 1883, "don't work well in the transportation business."[29] More and more businessmen began to recognize that the economy did not—and could not—work according to the supposedly immutable laws of political economy. In 1889 Andrew Carnegie said that "political economy says that . . . goods will not be produced at less than cost. This was true when Adam Smith wrote, but it is not quite true today."[30] In any case, many businessmen had never been averse to some kinds of governmental intervention, especially laws that restricted competition in their favor. By the mid-1880s, many businessmen and many workingmen were coming to the same conclusion: The free competition of wages and prices was not sacrosanct doctrine. The year labor historians call the "great upheaval," 1884, saw many strikes, and from 1885 to 1886 the membership of the Knights of Labor jumped from about 100,-000 to 700,000. Although by the late 1880s unions were still regarded with suspicion by a majority of Americans, many states had passed a sizable body of labor legislation that provided machinery for arbitrating labor disputes, restricted hours of work for women and children, enforced safety standards in the factory, and protected wages in various ways.

Perhaps no reformer was more dismayed by the loss of faith in laissez faire than William Graham Sumner, a professor of social theory at Yale. Sumner was a true believer in Spencerian individualism; his essays, newspaper columns, and books were read with approval by reformers. The answer to his *What the Social Classes Owe Each Other* (1883) is: Nothing. "The fact that a man is here is no demand upon other people that they shall keep him alive and sustain him."[31] Sumner inveighed against all forms of governmen-

tal intervention, especially against protective tariffs, saying that such measures would inevitably lead to socialism. Like Godkin, he vehemently defended laissez faire, and he continually exhorted his readers to oppose every
departure from it as a betrayal of all that was best in American civilization.

Sumner was fighting a losing battle. By the mid-1880s the proponents
of laissez faire were increasingly on the defensive. Moreover, Sumner himself gave ammunition to those who questioned it, for he did not argue, as
Godkin did, that laissez faire was based on scientific truth. "It is a maxim
of policy," he said, "not a rule of science."[32] Sumner was acknowledging
a weakness in classic political theory that was soon seized upon. "One of
the most amusing absurdities of the period," one critic said, are those
writers "who lay so great a stress on the word *natural*. . . ." He claimed
that the word was devoid of meaning, and that one could just as easily say
that the social reformers who try to respond to new historical conditions
"are legitimate and necessary, nay, natural products of every country and
age. . . ."[33] Even if laissez faire were natural law, it made no sense to say
that the world must conform to it. There is no necessary harmony, several
writers argued, between natural law and human advantage; and in the late
1880s many social theorists began to realize that changing conditions required some modification of classical political economy.

Godkin, like most reformers, disagreed. The new economics, he argued,
was not legitimate political economy. It was the work of young university
teachers without experience, who were at bottom socialists. The *Nation*
continually attacked Richard Ely, the leading figure among the younger
economists, and when Ely left Johns Hopkins for the University of Wiscon-
sin, Godkin exulted. "Professors of Political Economy preaching their own
philanthropic gospel as 'science'," he wrote to the president of Johns Hopkins, "are among the most dangerous characters of our time, and Ely was
one of them."[34] Other reformers were of the same mind—one accusing Ely
of tampering with "God's plan of providence and government," another
arguing that Ely's teachings resembled "the ravings of an Anarchist or the
dreams of a Socialist."[35]

It is hard to say why the reformers, unlike many politicians and businessmen, remained opposed to any attempts to modify laissez faire. Perhaps it
was their very disinterestedness that rendered them so immune to criticisms
of their ideas. Their sense of themselves as the only public-spirited citizens
made it easy for them to dismiss those who questioned their views. Opponents were invariably scorned as narrow and self-interested, though sometimes they were attacked as dangerous utopians. Whatever the reason for
the reformers' rigidity, it left them high and dry, removed from the currents
of the time. As the Gilded Age progressed, "the best men" found themselves
less inclined to work for reform and more inclined to castigate the present,

to utter dire predictions about the future, and to praise a past when liberal individualism had flourished and their fathers had been deferred to as leaders of the country.

At first, however, the reformers were zealous advocates of particular reforms. Priding themselves on their disinterestedness, they wanted to banish self-interest from politics—or at least reduce its influence—and they thought civil service reform the key to their efforts. Awarding federal jobs on the basis of competitive examinations, they thought, would have far-reaching effects; the caliber of federal employees would improve significantly. As early as 1866, Godkin had called for a purge of the civil service, the removal of "political partisans destitute of business capacity" as well as "political eunuchs with not force enough to call their souls their own."[36] And in 1869 Henry Adams, in the *North American Review,* called upon President Grant to use his executive power to institute a system of competitive examinations. "If the Administration will only frame a sound policy of reform, we shall gravitate towards it like iron filings to a magnet."[37] Grant did not heed the call, for his first annual message to Congress made no mention of civil service reform. Nevertheless, the reformers persisted in their efforts, for virtually all of them were convinced that civil service reform was the central issue of the day.

Civil service reform was anathema to most professional politicians. "Politics are impossible without the spoils," Richard Croker of Tammany said. "It is very well to argue that it ought not to be so. But we have to deal with men as they are, and with things as they are."[38] The spoils system, the professional politicians asserted, was both democratic and in the public interest. It enabled men of all backgrounds to assume the burdens and responsibilities of public service, and it prevented a tenured bureaucracy from being able to thwart the will of elected officials. Moreover, if there was no possibility of reward for services rendered, many people would be reluctant to devote any time to political work. The spoils system, it was claimed, was a form of civic education, giving people the chance to learn about the distinctive complexities of political life. So Andrew Jackson had argued in 1829, and so Grover Cleveland implied in 1884: "I have no sympathy with the intolerant people who, without the least appreciation of the meaning of party work and service, superciliously affect to despise all those who apply for office as they would those guilty of a flagrant misdemeanor."[39]

But a system that may have made sense in Jackson's time, when there were only 20,000 persons on the federal payroll, made less sense in Cleveland's, when there were 131,000. Dividing the spoils became increasingly difficult and unwieldy, consuming an inordinate amount of time and resulting in feuds between the president and selected members of Congress. Lincoln, Grant, Hayes, Garfield, and Cleveland all complained about the time they had to spend with office seekers. "The fountains of the population seem to have overflowed and Washington is inundated,"[40] Garfield complained three days after his inauguration, when they swarmed into the White House, harassing his wife as well. Many Americans—including professional politicians—thought the spoils system needed to be modified if not done away altogether. Starting with a new slate every four years was extraordinarily inefficient, and more and more federal jobs required special skills that made them unsuitable for spoilsmen.

After having been ignored by the Grant administration, the reformers learned to their elation that both candidates for the presidency in 1876 were in favor of civil service reform. Tilden spoke of how he had attacked the spoils system in New York; Hayes called for a "thorough, radical and complete reform of the civil service." For once Godkin found himself in the unusual position of bestowing praise upon a politician: "Nothing is more remarkable or more cheering than the position they both take up with regard to the reform of the civil service."[41] Hayes was genuinely committed to reform. In his diary he noted: "Now for civil service reform. Legislation must be prepared and executive rules and maxims. We must limit and narrow the area of patronage. We must diminish the evils of office-seeking."[42] But he had little influence with a Congress that was, for the most part, opposed to reform; little influence with key members of his own party, one of whom sneered at him for being a "political dreamer." Because he did not think that patronage could be limited by executive order, his hands were tied. He did, however, issue an order that forbade officeholders from participating in the management of party affairs, and he also abolished the practice of levying monetary assessments upon them.

The reformers were not inclined to appreciate Hayes's difficulties. They expected executive action because they thought civil service reform an urgent matter. "Unless we can reform the civil service," one reformer forecasted, "the country will go to the dogs."[43] Reformers thought any temporizing on the part of Hayes was a sign that he was caving in to professional politicians, that he might be a "jelly-fish," the term they used for politicians who hesitated to vote decisively for or against the party machine. Garfield was regarded with a similar distrust, even though he had been outspoken about the need for civil service reform. The distrust heightened when he said in 1880 that he supported the Republican platform, which barely alluded to civil service reform. Carl Schurz, a noted reformer, warned Garfield that "independent elements" in the party might defect unless he took a strong stand on the matter. Irritated that reformers thought he had surrendered to the machine, Garfield pointed out that his own views did not coincide with those of many Republicans: "There are real differences among Republicans."[44] Such restraint, the reformers thought, was backsliding, a sign that Garfield was tainted with "professionalism." Although most reformers voted for Garfield, they were lukewarm in their support. Whatever his views on civil service, he was a professional politician and therefore could not be trusted. After all, he had accepted as his running mate Chester Arthur, a protégé of Senator Roscoe Conkling's, who was a strong advocate of the spoils system.

Like Hayes, Garfield was wholeheartedly for civil service reform. He noted in his diary that "in some way the civil service must be regulated by law, or the president can never devote his time to administration."[45] But the presidency during the Gilded Age was a weak office, and the president rarely could command party support on measures he favored. Yet, what Garfield could not accomplish by wielding the power of the presidency eventually was accomplished by the "power" of his death. In 1881 he was assassinated by a demented spoilsman—an admirer of Senator Conkling who had gone to Washington as a Republican office seeker and been rebuffed. "We do not think," the *Nation* said soon after Garfield had been shot, "we have taken up a newspaper during the last ten days which has not in some manner made the crime the product of 'the spoils system.' "[46] Despite public opinion, professional politicians were still reluctant to overthrow the spoils system, but the congressional elections of 1882 made it clear that those congressmen who stoutly resisted civil service reform would be turned out of office. The Pendleton bill, which was signed by President Arthur on 16 January 1883, was passed by large, nonpartisan majorities, but many congressmen disliked it, even some who were responsible for its passage. "We are not legislating on this subject in response to our own judgment," one senator said, "but in response to some sort of judgment which has been expressed outside."[47] Although the reformers were disappointed by the modest nature of the bill, which designated only fifteen thousand jobs to be filled by competitive examinations, they were gleeful that public opinion was on their side. "Congress is like a pack of whipped boys this winter," Mrs. Henry Adams wrote to a friend; and Adams himself remarked that the average congressman was "chiefly occupied in swearing at professional reformers and voting for their bills."[48] For the first time, the reformers' efforts had met with some success.

Some congressmen, as Adams was well aware, were vitriolic in their hatred of reformers who had forced them to make some accommodation with the spirit of reform. But many found themselves admitting—albeit grudgingly—that some reform in the civil service was needed. In the Senate debate on the Pendleton bill, a Republican senator warned colleagues not only that "the public sentiment has come to absolutely demand it" but also that "the necessities of the case demand it; for with the growth of the country to 55 million people, and the growth of the list of appointees up to more than 100,000, it is quite obvious that in a short time this business of peddling patronage will absolutely crush every executive department."[49] Efficiency demanded that at least some federal jobs not be subject to rotation every four years.

All congressmen desired efficient government, but efficiency was not the only criterion to be invoked when weighing the merits of civil service reform. The reformers notwithstanding, the fact that many congressmen wanted to keep the spoils system relatively intact cannot be ascribed to venality or narrow self-interest. Some Democrats opposed the Pendleton bill because they thought it a bill to perpetuate in office the Republicans who controlled the patronage, but most senators opposed a dramatic reduction in the spoils system on less partisan grounds: They feared that such reforms would lead to "an aristocracy of office-holders," as an editorial in the *New York Sun* said, an aristocracy similar to the one in Prussia and China. Such a ruling class would be culled for the most part from the well-educated, who would score the highest on competitive examinations.[50] Chester Arthur worried that "mere intellectual proficiency" would be exalted above other qualities, and that experienced men would be at a disadvantage in competition with recent college graduates.[51] Civil service reform, in short, would put "the best men" in control of the federal bureaucracy, and would make them relatively immune from congressional control. A civil service system totally divorced from party patronage would be a threat to democratic government.

Such were the fears of many thoughtful politicians. The fears had some basis in reality, for "the best men" hoped to reap the rewards of civil service reform. The rewards were deserved, so "the best men" said, because they alone were disinterested patriots who knew what was best for the country. In "Civil Service Reform," Henry Adams contrasts two members of Grant's administration: one a professional politician, the other one of "the best men." Secretary of the Treasury Boutwell is "the product of caucusses and party promotion," but Attorney General Hoar is "by birth and training a representative of the best New England school. . . . Judge Hoar belonged in fact to a class of men who had been gradually driven from politics, but whom it is the hope of reformers to restore."[52] Praising the Judge Hoars, Adams claims that only such people are truly disinterested. The claim was one that the professional politicians readily conceded, for only the reformers said that they stood on the high ground of disinterest; the professional politicians preferred the lesser elevation of enlightened self-interest. As George Washington Plunkitt of Tammany Hall said: All the professional politicians were agreed "on the main proposition that when a man works in politics, he should get something out of it."[53] Adams maintained that "the best men" had been driven from politics, but it is more accurate to say that they left by themselves, in dislike of the fact that the professional politicians were a "class of men" who did not agree with their principles.

Despite their contempt for professional politicians, the reformers wanted to wield political influence if not necessarily hold political power. Flushed with the modest success of civil service reform, they thought they were more influential than they really were. And they were encouraged in their illusions by Cleveland's victory in 1884. The reformers claimed that their support—the support, that is, of those who had bolted the Republican party because they abhorred James Blaine, its presidential candidate—had given Cleveland the election. The Mugwumps, as the bolters were called, thought they would be influential because Cleveland was aware of how much he owed his election to their support. Moreover, they thought Cleveland was on their side. During the campaign, Godkin spoke glowingly of Cleveland, calling him a statesman comparable in integrity and stature to the greatest men in the nation's past. Cleveland would do his own thinking and be his own master.[54] But the reformers' illusions were soon shattered, for the pressures and constraints of the presidency would not have allowed Cleveland to perform according to their lights even if he had wanted to.

Before becoming disillusioned with Cleveland, the reformers had to contend with another distressing fact: The election of 1884 had split "the party of the center" in two. Some reformers, fearing the Democratic party and distrusting Cleveland, decided to support Blaine despite their misgivings about him. The Mugwumps regarded those who stayed in the Republican fold as unprincipled. Godkin was his usual vitriolic self: "We say deliberately," he wrote in the *Nation*, "that greater disgrace than these men are today inflicting on American Government and society has not been witnessed in modern times."[55] Such virulent attacks naturally did not go down well with those reformers who had not bolted the Republican party. Reformers such as Henry Cabot Lodge and Theodore Roosevelt thought the Mugwumps' uncompromising highmindedness would forever make them ineffectual. As Lodge said: "Since I gave up trying to make a rope of sand—an independent party composed exclusively of good men—I have been in the school of party politics and the lesson I have learned there practically at least is to show some liberality toward those who differ from me."[56] Having become a professional politician, Lodge had acquired a trait rarely possessed by reformers: a willingness to entertain views that differed from his own.

If the Mugwumps were especially angered by the actions of some of "the best men," they were sorely disappointed by Cleveland. Godkin had assured his readers that Cleveland would remove no one from the federal government "on account of his political opinions," but by July 1886 Cleveland had decided that 90 percent of the government officeholders under his direct control were "incompetent," and had fired most of the officials not covered by the Pendleton Act—not because they were incompetent but because they were Republicans. One reformer commented that the "President seems to think he has to stoop down for the purpose of lifting up his party to his level. . . . The danger is that he who thus stoops down may not be able to quite straighten up again himself."[57] In a sense, the reformer was right: Cleveland had to stoop down. The Mugwumps may have helped him carry the election, but they constituted only a fraction—and a potentially disloyal one at that—of a party that had been out of power for some time, a party that certainly did not want to "play fair" and let the Republicans keep the spoils. Assigning the spoils, however, was a chore that Cleveland—like Lincoln, Grant, Hayes, and Garfield—disliked: "The d——d everlasting clatter for the offices continues to some extent," he wrote friends, "and makes me feel like resigning. . . ."[58] But it was a chore he could not refuse if he wanted to have some influence within his own party.

The early history of civil service reform, then, is a peculiar tale. The "party of the center" got nowhere with its efforts until a crazed spoilsman, a self-confessed admirer of Senator Roscoe Conkling, shot President Garfield. The assassination put a protégé of Conkling's in the presidency, but it also destroyed the influence of Conkling, a man who hated reformers, and made the electorate clamor for civil service reform. And in two years, President Chester Arthur, who had once been a masterly spoilsman, found himself signing into law the first civil service reform act. Once the act was passed, there was little enthusiasm for it, especially in Congress, but the number of jobs under civil service classification steadily increased. To prevent his own spoilsmen from losing their jobs, every president made additions to the classified list near the end of his term—a process that was hastened by the alternation of party control during the 1880s and 1890s. Thus professional politicians abetted civil service reform, but for reasons the reformers despised.

The reformers welcomed the progress of civil service reform, however anomalous it was, but the political landscape of the late 1880s did not gladden their hearts. The professional politician was gaining rather than losing influence. Moreover, Cleveland himself had sorely disappointed them. "Cleveland's course," a prominent reformer wrote in 1887, "has left all of us Mugwumps in an apparently disagreeable position. . . . It has certainly discredited civil service reform and chilled those who were his most earnest supporters in 1884."[59] But it was more than Cleveland's course or the continuing strength of the political machines that chilled the reformers. By the end of the decade the reforms they had ardently pursued had become dead issues. Most Americans had lost interest in civil service reform, and most Americans no longer rallied to laissez faire. The corporate world, many thought, should be regulated, and in 1887 the Interstate Commerce Act became law, followed in 1890 by the Sherman Antitrust Act. The reformers were beginning to feel irrelevant.

But there was one issue for which the reformers had a receptive audience: immigration policy. Like many Americans, the reformers feared that unrestricted immigration would be ruinous to the polity. Immigrant politics meant machine politics, the politics of the urban boss who catered to the needs of new immigrants, providing services and jobs in return for blocs of votes. In the 1880s the new immigrants, who came increasingly from Southern and Eastern Europe, bolstered the power of professional politicians. According to the reformers, the immigrants were making a sham of representative government. Americans, they thought, had to become aware of the danger at hand, aware that every political and industrial disturbance of the decade was the work of immigrants, whose foreign ways and foreign ideas were undermining the Republic.

No one sounded the alarm more persistently than E. L. Godkin. The railroad strike of 1877, the *Nation* said, was "a national disgrace" that portended "a widespread rising, not against political oppression or unpopular government, but against society itself."[60] Although Godkin claimed that he was not against unions that respected the "rules of morality," he violently attacked all efforts by unions to be more than social organizations. Labor legislation, he said, would pave the way for communism. All such agitation —a favorite word of Godkin's—was the fault of the immigrants who were swarming to the United States to advance their "wild desire and wilder dreams." By "agitation" Godkin meant even the movement for an eight-hour day—a movement he branded as foreign in origin, brought by men who believed in the "odious despotism of a secret, oath-bound 'union'."[61] Godkin was most disturbed by the closed shop, which he rightly regarded as an abridgment of the worker's freedom to bargain independently with the employer. But Godkin had little understanding or appreciation of the industrial worker's plight that made inevitable his banding together with other workers to create an effective bargaining force. The *Nation* never called for an antitrust prosecution of an employers' association or an industrial monopoly, but it frequently called for government action against trade unions.

Perhaps because of his isolated position in New York, where reformers were fewer and had much less influence than in Massachusetts, Godkin was more intemperate than most reformers in his attack on the unholy trio of immigrants, labor agitators, and professional politicians. Although William James declared that he owed his "whole political education" to Godkin and considered him a fount of political wisdom, James was not so gloomy about the rise of labor. Writing to his brother in 1886, he argued that labor troubles "are a most healthy phase of evolution, a little costly, but normal, and sure to do lots of good to all hands in the end."[62] Yet, James's optimism was distinctly untypical. More reformers were closer to the position of Lyman Atwater, a reformist minister who called strikes "conspiracies against the laws of God, the rights of man, and the welfare of society" and warned that the importation of the "dregs" of Europe was engendering widespread social disorder.[63]

The reformers were not the only Americans who feared the so-called dregs from abroad. A strong current of nativism runs through the politics of the 1880s and 1890s, aggravated probably by the depression of the early 1890s. Not only reformers would have assented to Charles Eliot Norton's remark in 1884 that "it does not look as if the better elements of social life, of human nature, were growing in proportion to the baser."[64] The baser elements were clearly the new immigrants, who flooded American cities in the last two decades of the century. (More than 6.3 million foreigners entered the United States between 1877 and 1890.) Nativist feelings were especially acute after 3 May 1886, when an unknown person threw a bomb at policemen in Chicago's Haymarket Square. The policemen had been breaking up a meeting of strikers that had been called by a small group of anarchists. The riot that ensued resulted in the arrest of eight suspects— arrested, apparently, only because they were known anarchists—who were eventually convicted of murder and hanged. Many Americans were convinced, as one minister said, that the "horrible tyranny was wholly of foreign origin." And numerous newspapers denounced the "scum and offal of Europe" for bringing socialism, anarchy, disorder, violence, and bomb-throwing to the United States. Godkin, who praised the trial and hanging, went one step further: Attacking the anarchists, he also attacked those American "social philosophers" who were preaching foreign ideas that encouraged the "dangerous classes" to conspire against liberal individualism. "Some of them have gone and are going far to share in the bloodguiltiness of this diabolical Anarchist agitation."[65]

Toward the end of the century nativism abated somewhat. The country was well on its way to economic recovery, and foreign workers were needed to make sure that industry continued its rapid development. Nevertheless, nativism remained quite virulent at times. On 10 September 1897, a sheriff's posse opened fire on striking coal miners at Lattimer, Pennsylvania, leaving nineteen dead and sixty wounded. According to witnesses, the posse had not been provoked, for there had been no violence on the part of the miners, who were all recent Slavic immigrants. The ninety-odd deputies were indicted for murder, but they were acquitted by a jury that heard the counsel for the defense call the miners a "barbarian horde" as well as declare that "the history of the Hun and the Slav in the old country is that of mischief and destruction." Most of the press, which continued to regard unions as carriers of foreign ideas that were subversive of American civilization, praised the verdict as "a triumph for order and civilization."[66]

On the question of immigration, then, the reformers were in the mainstream of public opinion—especially in the late eighties and early nineties when, as one historian says, "the whole nation was beginning to worry about the same thing."[67] The concern, however, produced only a trickle of legislation, and none that significantly restricted immigration. In 1882, Congress passed a law that suspended Chinese immigration for ten years and also denied admission to convicts, lunatics, idiots, and persons likely to become a public charge. In 1885, it passed a law that forbade prepayment of transportation of an immigrant in return for a promise of services. In the early 1890s the concern about immigration became acute, and in 1894 a group of Boston patricians founded the Immigration Restriction League to alert the country to the social and economic dangers of the new immigration. In Congress, restrictionist legislation sponsored by the Immigration Restriction League was put forward by Henry Cabot Lodge. The bill was especially popular with reformers, for it would have excluded all male adults unable to read and write their own language. Such a test, it was hoped, would have the influx from Southern and Eastern Europe. The bill passed easily through a Congress that was controlled by the Republicans but it was vetoed by Cleveland as one of his last acts in office. Legislation to restrict immigration was not enacted until 1917.

Given the public temper, why was the effort to restrict immigration not more successful? It failed in part because it was not in the interest of many businessmen. The great expansion and simplification of factory processes made it imperative that unskilled labor be readily available, and both the National Association of Manufacturers and the Chamber of Commerce lobbied vigorously against restriction. The effort failed also because the Democratic party was never strongly in favor of restricting immigration, because the party relied heavily on the votes of immigrants to retain power in the large industrial cities of the Northeast and Midwest. Another reason may be the most important: Many Americans ranted against the dregs of Europe, but many were also proud that their country had always been a refuge for those fleeing the poverty and oppression of the Old World. Restrictionist legislation was, to their minds, unpatriotic; it went against the American grain. Moreover, if in the past immigrants had been assimilated, perhaps those coming from Southern and Eastern Europe could also be assimilated. Only the reformers took a consistently gloomy view of the new immigration; only the reformers were certain that the swarms of illiterate Italians, Jews, and Slavs would prove fatal to representative government.

The reformers were never noted for vacillation. To change one's view was a sign at best of caving in to public opinion, at worst of actually being corrupt. It was letting sound principles be tarnished by the confusion and venality of political life. Reflecting upon the role of the reformer, Charles Francis Adams pontificated: "At a mighty interval with unequal steps we are the followers of Copernicus and Galileo and Bacon and Newton and Adam Smith and Bentham. How does it concern us that the mass—the mighty majority—of our fellow voters are ignorant and stupid and selfish and short-sighted? That's the practical statesman's affair."[68] Indeed it was: Professional politicians had no choice but to be shortsighted. They could not afford to remain attached to "sound principles" because they had to come up with policies that were, above all, politically expedient. Although Cleveland considered himself a supporter of laissez faire, he realized that the country would suffer if capital and labor continued on their collision course. "Our workingmen are not asking unreasonable indulgence," he said in his letter of acceptance in 1884. And a year after taking office, he asked Congress to establish a permanent labor commission that would be charged with "the consideration and settlement, when possible" of all controversies between labor and capital.[69]

Forced to be shortsighted, professional politicians were also forced to have wider views. Their working conditions made it impossible for them to rely on such abstractions as laissez faire when dealing with the groups that composed their constituency. Many businessmen also came to realize that it was not expedient to invoke laissez faire when faced with the demands of labor. Mark Hanna said of George Pullman, whose obduracy touched off the destructive railroad strike of 1894: "A man who won't meet his men half-way is a God-damn fool!" And Boise Penrose told Henry C. Frick, the head of Carnegie Steel: "What is the use of shooting a man for striking? Compromise with him. Give him half what he demands. That will be twice as much as he expects to get."[70] Many politicians and businessmen scrambled to reach some sort of compromise, but the reformers stood firm. Certain that their views were both morally and intellectually correct, they found it difficult to see things in a new light. Furious with the refusal of Congress to enact legislation that conformed to the principles of laissez faire, Edward Atkinson, a noted reformer, complained that "bad laws are making knaves faster than preachers can make saints."[71]

Atkinson was a resolute defender of laissez faire, but he was not hard-hearted. A man of genuine good will, he wanted to find some way to help the poor without sapping their self-reliance. In 1892 he came up with the Aladdin Oven, a species of pressure cooker that produced nutritious meals at allegedly phenomenal savings. The Aladdin Oven, Atkinson claimed, would enable the poor to spend their money wisely; the money they saved would enable them to live in comfort. Atkinson hoped that his oven would

check the pernicious influence of unions, and he advertised it as a remedy
for socialism. Workers, of course, were not impressed. "Political economy
is one branch of human knowledge, cookery another," a labor leader said.
"We want the best of each, but not both together."[72]

Atkinson's remedy for the disease of unions is an extreme example of the
reformers' inability to understand the forces at work in the new industrial
order. Perhaps some reformers were, as Samuel Tilden said, men "of
pecuniary independence and leisure" who had selfishly abdicated their
power of leadership and had no right, therefore, to criticize the immigrant
element in politics.[73] But most reformers were simply prisoners of their own
highmindedness, which made it impossible for them to see that all devia-
tions from the straight and narrow path of liberal individualism were not
necessarily subversive of democracy. Reformers like Godkin and Atkinson
did not grasp what was obvious to professional politicians like Cleveland
and Tilden: Most workers wanted what other Americans had—better
wages, shorter hours, and safer working conditions. Most workers also
wanted some acknowledgment that they had a right to raise these demands.

The reformers admitted that workers—especially if they were new immigrants—were often treated harshly by employers, but the reformers' sound
principles of political economy rendered them incapable of grappling with
the question of worker rights. All they could do was either scold employers
for being too greedy or warn workers about the dangers of drink, laziness,
and prodigality. The workers ignored such patronizing; they knew that the
only way they could help themselves was by banding together. Perhaps
because the new immigrants usually came from villages where the notion
of liberal individualism had never held sway, they were incapable of American self-reliance. Such was the line taken by many pessimistic reformers.
But the new industrial order made it likely that any worker—no matter
what his background—would resort to collective action to get a better deal
from his employer.

Eschewing all forms of collective action, the reformers increasingly were
ineffectual outsiders. They kept themselves "free from entangling alliances,"[74] as one Mugwump put it, at a time when such alliances were
becoming commonplace—when Americans of all stripe, from farmers to
professors, were deciding that it was in their interest to join organizations.
By the end of the century, even the political parties became more cohesive.
According to David Rothman, the post–Civil War years should not be
remembered as the age of corruption but as the age of organization, "the
start of the modern system by which pressure groups vied for government
support."[75]

By the 1890s the reformers sensed that they were swimming against the
current, but they remained proud of their exertions, which they considered

a sign of their civic courage. "In a country so constituted as ours," one among their number said, "there are few deeds more admirable than that of the public man who, devoted to a principle, is willing unflinchingly to face a hostile majority."[76] It was but a short step, however, from courageously questioning whether the majority was always in the right to smugly believing that the majority was always in the wrong. "When I am in a small minority I believe I am right," one reformer said. "When I am in a minority of one, I know I am right."[77] The reformers proudly stood their ground, upholding their principles but not examining them. As they moved into old age, their capacity to deplore matters increased at the expense of their capacity to reflect upon matters.

In short, the reformers turned sour, their disillusion extending even to democracy. In 1892, a prominent reformer expressed admiration for Alexander Hamilton "and his scorn of the spurious Democracy which is always found in all American parties."[78] Godkin had similar thoughts; in 1896, he predicted "very evil times" for democracy. Two years before, he had commented to Charles Eliot Norton: "About democracy . . . I have pretty much given it up as a contribution to the world's moral progress. . . ." Many reformers agreed, and one praised Godkin for his "appreciation of the progressive political and civic degeneracy . . . in this country."[79]

The reformers' despair was by no means completely unjustified. We cannot dismiss their loss of faith in democracy as merely the resentment of men whose status no longer was what it had been, men who no longer were deferred to as "the best men" of the country. The reformers were, to some degree, right: Politics in the late nineteenth century—especially immigrant politics—was a disturbing business. If most politicians were not corrupt— did not, that is, take bribes—many did manipulate elections. In the late 1880s, more than a third of the states allowed persons not yet naturalized to vote, and in others the fraudulent registration of aliens was common. Moreover, most of the new immigrants who came from Southern and Eastern Europe had virtually no understanding of representative government. Immigrants, James Bryce said in *The American Commonwealth* (1888), "follow blindly leaders of their own race, are not moved by discussion, [and] exercise no judgment of their own." And he added that "they know nothing of the institutions of the country, of its statesmen, of its political issues."[80] Many Americans, not only the reformers, worried about the effect so many aliens would have on American democracy.

What distinguishes the reformers from most Americans is not their fear of aliens or even their rigid adherence to laissez faire. It is their refusal to countenance the notion that self-interest should play a part in politics. Preaching a politics of disinterest, the reformers cut themselves off from most Americans, not only from professional politicians, for expressions of self-interest were regarded as perfectly legitimate. Self-interest was a major ingredient in the deliberative process that resulted in the regulation of "various and interfering interests."

Tinkering with the system, adjusting it so that it could better meet the needs of a new industrial age, professional politicians usually did not pause to speculate about the motives of someone advancing an idea. They assumed that self-interest was the engine that produced most ideas and they cared only that the idea was a good one. The reformers, the strident defenders of laissez faire, never understood the reason for laissez faire, which was to tap the energy latent in self-interest. Only the reformers disliked the entrepreneurial spirit, a spirit that informed American politics as well as American business.

Professional politicians—corrupt or not—had a better sense than the reformers of what the age required because they were attuned to public opinion. "Too much stress cannot be laid," Bryce said, "that the strong point of the American system . . . is the healthiness of public opinion, and the control which it exerts."[81] It was public clamor against election frauds that led most state governments in the 1890s to adopt the Australian ballot, an electoral method in which uniform ballots were prepared and distributed by the state and then cast in secret. This procedure significantly limited the ability of political machines to manipulate electoral results. Many professional politicians may have been "hardboiled," even cynical, but they respected public opinion and closely followed it. The reformers disavowed it.

The reformers, as we have seen, also scorned political parties. One Mugwump said of Cleveland: "He is strong, not because of his party, but despite it."[82] Throughout the 1880s and 1890s, they hoped that the parties would disintegrate. Yet, if the parties fraudulently registered immigrants, they also attended to the needs of immigrants without talking down to them. And they also enabled the sons of immigrants to gain access to power through a career in politics. Because the worlds of banking and big business were usually closed to immigrants as well as to the sons of immigrants, politics offered them one of the few avenues to success.

Parties also served another function. In *The American Commonwealth*, Bryce is astounded by "the peculiar gift which the Republic possesses of quickly dissolving and assimilating the foreign bodies that are poured into her mass, imparting to them her own qualities of orderliness, good sense, self-restraint, a willingness to bow to the will of the majority. . . ."[83] Bryce ascribes the transformation to the force of public opinion as it was felt in the schools, the factories, and the newspapers, but surely many immigrants were so quickly assimilated because they participated in local politics. With its complex organization, the party was a school in itself, a school in which immigrants acquired a civic education. The reformers were right to criticize some aspects of machine politics, but they were blind to the positive aspects of parties. The parties helped to turn immigrants into citizens; and the parties, by enabling special interests to find some common denominator within the fold of the party, acted to "break and control the violence of faction."

One does not want to make great claims for the professional politicians of the Gilded Age. In general, they were not an inspiring lot, but we can say that they enabled the extended commercial republic to work better than it would have if the reformers had been deferred to as "the best men." Standing upon their disinterest, as it were, the reformers were immune to public opinion and unreceptive to criticisms of their ideas. Professional politicians were certainly less cultivated and less well read than the reformers, but they were much more receptive to new ideas. And because they were more open minded, they were more capable of finding ways of averting violent faction. It would be extreme to call the reformers dangerous to the health of the Republic, but we can say that their principled approach to politics, like that of the Federalists of the 1790s, made them a divisive force. And we can also say that the country would have suffered a good deal more turmoil if professional politicians had remained as committed to laissez faire as the reformers were.

After looking at the Federalists of the 1790s and the "party of the center" of the 1870s and 1880s, can we not conclude that the politics of disinterest undermines Publius's science of politics because those who stand upon their disinterest regard the claims of special interests as illegitimate and therefore unworthy of their attention? If so, it may be that the growth of a politics of disinterest constitutes more of a threat to the health of the American form of representative government than the power of special interests. To test this assumption, we should look at another age in which the politics of disinterest flourished: the 1970s.

Notes

1. John G. Sproat, *"The Best Men": Liberal Reformers in the Gilded Age* (New York: Oxford University Press, 1968), p. 90.
2. Cited, Ari Hoogenboom, *Outlawing the Spoils: A History of the Civil Service Movement, 1865–1883* (Urbana: University of Illinois Press, 1961), p. 39.
3. Cited, Morton Keller, *Affairs of State: Public Life in Late Nineteenth Century America* (Cambridge: Harvard University Press, 1977), p. 290.
4. Cited, Sproat, *"The Best Men"*, p. 101.
5. *The Education of Henry Adams* (New York: Random House, 1931), p. 272.
6. Cited, H. Wayne Morgan, *From Hayes to McKinley: National Party Politics, 1877–1896* (Syracuse: Syracuse University Press, 1969), p. 37.
7. *Education of Henry Adams*, pp. 280–81.

8. Ibid.
9. "The New York Gold Conspiracy," in *A Henry Adams Reader,* ed. Elizabeth Stevenson (Garden City: Doubleday Anchor, 1959), pp. 84–85.
10. David Rothman, *Politics and Power: The United States Senate, 1869–1901* (Cambridge: Harvard University Press, 1966), p. 153.
11. Ibid., p. 201.
12. Cited, John A. Garraty, *The New Commonwealth: 1877–1890* (New York: Harper & Row, 1968), p. 234.
13. Ibid., pp. 233–35.
14. Ibid., p. 240.
15. Cited, Morgan, *From Hayes to McKinley,* p. 273.
16. Cited, Garraty, *New Commonwealth,* pp. 249, 238.
17. Cited, Keller, *Affairs of State,* p. 194.
18. Morgan, *From Hayes to McKinley,* p. 531.
19. Cited, ibid., p. 27.
20. Ibid., p. 56.
21. Cited, Sproat, *"The Best Men",* p. 164.
22. Cited, Garraty, *New Commonwealth,* p. 158.
23. Cited, Sproat, *"The Best Men",* pp. 163, 146.
24. Cited, Garraty, *New Commonwealth,* p. 28.
25. See Sproat, *"The Best Men",* p. 152.
26. Cited, Donald Fleming, "Social Darwinism," in *Paths of American Thought,* ed. Arthur M. Schlesinger, Jr., and Morton White (Boston: Houghton Mifflin, 1963), pp. 124–25.
27. Cited, Richard Hofstadter, *Social Darwinism in American Thought* (Boston: Beacon Press, 1955), p. 89.
28. Ibid., pp. 47–48.
29. Cited, Garraty, *New Commonwealth,* p. 109.
30. Ibid.
31. Cited, Max Lerner, "The Triumph of Laissez-Faire," in Schlesinger, Jr., and White, *Paths of American Thought,* p. 156.
32. Ibid.
33. Cited, Hofstadter, *Social Darwinism,* p. 80.
34. Cited, Geoffrey Blodgett, *The Gentle Reformers: Massachusetts Democrats in the Cleveland Era* (Cambridge: Harvard University Press, 1966), p. 76.
35. Cited, Sproat, *"The Best Men",* p. 156.
36. Cited, Hoogenboom, *Outlawing the Spoils,* p. 19.
37. Ibid., p. 68.
38. Cited, Morgan, *From Hayes to McKinley,* p. 252.
39. Ibid., p. 251.
40. Ibid., p. 128.
41. Cited, Hoogenboom, *Outlawing the Spoils,* pp. 143–44.
42. Ibid., p. 151.
43. Ibid., p. 138.
44. Cited, Sproat, *"The Best Men",* p. 108.
45. Cited, Morgan, *From Hayes to McKinley,* p. 162.
46. Cited, Hoogenboom, *Outlawing the Spoils,* p. 209.
47. Ibid., p. 251.
48. Ibid., pp. 236, 252.
49. Cited, Morgan, *From Hayes to McKinley,* p. 163.

50. Ibid.
51. Cited, Richard Hofstadter, *Anti-Intellectualism in American Life* (New York: Random House, 1963), p. 185.
52. Cited, Hoogenboom, *Outlawing the Spoils,* p. 67.
53. Cited, Richard Hofstadter, *The Age of Reform* (New York: Alfred A. Knopf, 1955), p. 184.
54. See Sproat, *"The Best Men",* p. 129.
55. Cited, ibid., p. 131.
56. Ibid., p. 272.
57. Cited, Morgan, *From Hayes to McKinley,* p. 253.
58. Ibid.
59. Cited, Hoogenboom, *Outlawing the Spoils,* p. 261.
60. Cited, Morgan, *From Hayes to McKinley,* p. 26.
61. Cited, Sproat, *"The Best Men",* p. 231.
62. Cited, Hofstadter, *Social Darwinism,* p. 134.
63. Cited, Keller, *Affairs of State,* p. 190.
64. Cited, Geoffrey Blodgett, "The Mind of the Boston Mugwump," in *Political Parties in American History, 1828–1890,* vol. 2, ed. Felice A. Bonadio (New York: G. P. Putnam's Sons, 1974), p. 887.
65. Cited, Sproat, *"The Best Men",* p. 234.
66. Cited, Arch Puddington, review of Michael Novak, *The Guns of Lattimer, Commentary* (March 1979): 96.
67. John Higham, "The Politics of Immigration Restriction," in *Send These to Me: Jews and Other Immigrants in Urban America* (New York: Atheneum, 1975), p. 37.
68. Cited, Blodgett, *Gentle Reformers,* p. 68.
69. Cited, Sproat, *"The Best Men",* p. 237.
70. Both Hanna and Penrose cited, Keller, *Affairs of State,* p. 540.
71. Cited, Blodgett, *Gentle Reformers,* p. 68.
72. Cited, Blodgett, "Mind of the Boston Mugwump," p. 891.
73. Cited, Sproat, *"The Best Men",* p. 256.
74. Cited, Blodgett, *Gentle Reformers,* p. 67.
75. Rothman, *Politics and Power,* p. 220.
76. Cited, Blodgett, "Mind of the Boston Mugwump," p. 896.
77. Cited, Morgan, *From Hayes to McKinley,* p. 29.
78. Cited, Hoogenboom, *Outlawing the Spoils,* p. 266.
79. Ibid.
80. James Bryce, *Selections from The American Commonwealth,* ed. Henry Steele Commager (New York: Fawcett, 1961), p. 90.
81. Ibid., p. 87.
82. Cited, Morgan, *From Hayes to McKinley,* p. 210.
83. Bryce, *Selections,* p. 91.

6
The 1970s: The Rise of Public Interest Groups

In 1970, approximately one hundred years after "the party of the center" was formed, John Gardner founded Common Cause, a self-proclaimed "citizens' lobby" that said it would be a third force in American life, a force that "would uphold the public interest against all comers—particularly against the special interests that dominate our national life today."[1] In less than four years, Common Cause became one of the biggest, best-organized, and best-financed lobbies in Washington, second in influence, according to one study, only to the AFL-CIO. Its membership reached 100,000 after twenty-three weeks and swelled to 324,000 after three years. Common Cause, as one observer says, "has written over the last decade an uncommon success story."[2] But Gardner's success was not unique; the early years of the 1970s witnessed the remarkable flowering of numerous organizations that proclaimed they were acting in the public interest. In addition to Common Cause, the most influential may have been the several public interest organizations subsumed under the rubric Public Citizen, which was founded by Ralph Nader in 1971.

It would be wrong to assume that all the public interest groups of the 1970s—despite their claims that they are upholding "the people's interest" —had the same agenda for change. By and large, Common Cause focused on regulating the political process, whereas Nader's organizations focused on regulating the corporation. "The nation is hurt," Gardner said, "when great decisions are made by venal men, concerned chiefly with private gain."[3] Nader has continually attacked "the overwhelming power of American corporations,"[4] and in 1979 he was instrumental in the formation of the Citizens party, which has called for "citizen control" of large corporations. Yet, often the agendas of Common Cause and Public Citizen have overlapped. Both organizations have played important roles in the passage of legislation on campaign financing and on open government.

But what is striking about the public interest movement of the 1970s is not the agendas but the influence it managed to acquire in a relatively short period of time. "Few private citizens," the *Wall Street Journal* claims of Gardner, "have had as lasting an impact on the governmental system as he."[5] During the early 1970s, Gardner and Nader were regarded as among the most powerful men in Washington and were seriously mentioned as possible presidential candidates. "The fact is," an official of the Carter administration commented in 1980, "the program advocated by the public interest movement in the early 1970s was passed." The movement was "wildly successful."[6]

Influence, of course, is not easy to assess, and it may be that the legislation Gardner and Nader lobbied for would have passed even if their organizations had not existed. In the early 1970s, especially after Watergate, public sentiment was on the side of regulating both the political process and the corporation. And, as Lincoln said: "With public sentiment on its side, everything succeeds; with public sentiment against it, nothing succeeds." There is no question that the public interest groups of the 1970s rode the wave of public sentiment, but it would be incorrect to assume that they were its passive beneficiaries. Both Gardner and Nader were expert manipulators of public opinion—adept in their relations with the press, adept also in their organizational tactics and lobbying strategies.

Nader had been the first to become an influential lobbyist. In the late 1960s, his fight for a number of measures designed to increase both consumer and worker safety had a favorable outcome. But it was Gardner who, in the summer of 1970, sensed that a sizable number of Americans were disenchanted with the political system and eager to work as volunteers for an organization dedicated to making government, as Gardner said, accountable to the people. It was Gardner, then, who first saw the possibility of creating a public interest organization with a mass base. Struck by Gardner's success, Nader followed suit in 1971.

By 1970 the war in Vietnam had cast a large shadow over American society. More than half the citizens opposed the war, but the opposition itself was divided. According to Godfrey Hodgson, there were two opposition "movements."[7] One was less a movement than a sprawling, inchoate mass of people from all walks of life who believed that the war was a mistake and had to stop. The other could more legitimately be labeled a movement, for it was composed of a numerically small though immensely influential body of people who thought the war was morally wrong and symptomatic as well of a deeper malaise that infected American society. The latter people were in the main from the upper middle class, professional elites: journalists, professors, policymakers, lawyers. Gardner was a member in good standing of this group, highly regarded "by the agenda setters and policy makers of Washington and New York."[8] And it was these people—as well as their sons and daughters—who provided the money and manpower for Common Cause and Public Citizen.

The disaffection of the professional elites was widespread. "I believe," Hedley Donovan, the editor-in-chief of *Time,* asserted in 1969, "the causes of our confusion go much deeper than Vietnam." And a writer in *Fortune* spoke of "the crisis of national perception," concluding that "the more passionate discussers of the four commanding topics of 1968—Vietnam, poverty, race, and law and order—regard each as a symptom of some deeper and more general moral sickness in contemporary U.S. society."[9] By 1970 the "passionate discussers" had become legion. Maynard Mack, a distinguished professor of English not theretofore known for radical sentiments, felt obliged in a lecture to the annual meeting of the Modern Language Association to speak of "our confused times" and lament that "we who have put a man on the moon cannot or will not open up our ghettos, pay the price in pride and probably in affluence that it takes to be rid of an offensive war." Mack also argued that "we aspire to the American Dream, but what we have got is the American Way, a society where the things that are not for sale grow fewer every year."[10]

Underlying Mack's words was the assumption that the United States was suffering from both an intolerable war and a surfeit of domestic problems because of corruption. The war was continuing, he implied, because some people were making money as a result of it. The United States is a society, he clearly suggested, where most things—by which he meant people—are for sale. The sentiment was pervasive among the professional elites, many of whom yoked corruption at home with the support of corrupt regimes abroad. Perhaps Frances FitzGerald's *Fire in the Lake,* published in 1972, was greeted with such acclaim because she made so much of corruption— hoping, she said, that the "narrow flame of revolution" might "cleanse the lake of Vietnamese society from the corruption and disorder of the American war."[11]

For the disaffected professional elites, the man who stood for all that was both corrupt and morally wrong was Richard Nixon. A man who had been, so it was said, an unscrupulous anti-Communist, a man who was reputed to be in league with the shadier elements of big business, Nixon was someone who could not be trusted. Nixon galvanized the disaffected elites. If he had not been president, it is doubtful that Common Cause and Public Citizen would have succeeded in raising so much money, attracting numerous volunteers, and hiring brilliant young lawyers for low pay. The fortunes of Common Cause and Public Citizen were inextricably tied to the career of Richard Nixon. Soon after Watergate, they reached the height of their influence, but as the Nixon era receded into the past their influence waned, so that in 1978 an observer could claim that "public interest groups are having a tough time making ends meet now that they don't have Dick Nixon to kick around anymore."[12] Common Cause's membership peaked at 325,000 on the day Nixon resigned; its budget in 1974 reached a high point of $6.9 million. In succeeding years, it lost more than 100,000 members, but in 1980 it reported a slight increase in its membership—perhaps owing to its new chairman, Archibald Cox, who had become a hero when he was fired by Nixon in the famous "Saturday night massacre." Public Citizen raised more than $1.3 million in 1977; a little less than $1 million in 1979.

In 1970 Nixon was very much around to kick. If he could not be blamed for the killings at Kent State, he could be blamed for the invasion of Cambodia, which occasioned many demonstrations on American campuses. The students at Yale might display, as its president, Kingman Brewster, said, a "monumental scorn"[13] for things as they are, but Gardner rightly sensed that the best and the brightest students as well as their affluent upper-middle-class parents would not be immune to the kind of appeal he was making, an appeal that said the American sickness could be cured if Americans dedicated themselves to cleaning up American politics —to making sure that the politicians were no longer unduly influenced by special interests. In mailings, Gardner and Nader harped on the notion of political corruption, implying that the political process favored, as Common Cause said, "the money-heavy special interests." And Nader continually warned that the people's interest was losing out to the monied interest. In short, both organizations couched their appeals for members or contributors (Public Citizen is not a membership organization) in similar terms.

As a spokesman for the "people's interest," Gardner was vulnerable to attack because "wealthy establishment bigwigs,"[14] in the words of one writer, had provided him with $250,000 in seed money for an initial membership drive that included many full-page newspaper advertisements as well as a direct-mail campaign that reached two and a half million persons. If, as Gardner himself repeatedly asserted, "Money talks . . . talks louder and longer and drowns out the citizen's hoarse whisper,"[15] then it seems that the Common Cause claim of being opposed to the "money-heavy special interests" was disingenuous. Such a charge, however, is unfair because Common Cause subsequently relied on membership dues for approximately 90 percent of its operating budget. Moreover, the support that Gardner received from some of the leading members of the business community was not a sign that Gardner was a fake reformer; it was a sign of the extent to which those businessmen were disaffected from the political system. Of course, they were not in favor of the "narrow flame of revolution," but they did want someone to clean up political corruption. Gardner seemed the right doctor, they thought, for America's sickness. They were more suspicious of Nader, but Nader had not turned to the corporate world for seed money to start Public Citizen. Although both Nader and Gardner had received contributions from Jack Dreyfus, the chairman of the Dreyfus Fund, most of the $314,000 Nader spent in 1971 to raise $1.1 million came out of his own pocket.

Both Gardner and Nader—as well as public interest groups in general—have been more vulnerable to criticism on another ground: They have been beholden not to the business and financial establishment but to their membership, which is by no means a cross-section of the people. According to this reasoning, the notion that Common Cause, for example, lobbies for "the people" is misguided; it lobbies for the interests of its membership, well-to-do white-collar workers "who have no organized interest group to lobby in their behalf, and who thus have every reason to dilute the strength of 'special interests' whose aims clash with their own."[16] Another critic calls Common Cause a "special interest" that advances the interests of "a comparatively small clerical class of bureaucrats, professors and public interest lawyers. . . ."[17] Even an observer generally well disposed toward public interest groups remarks that "the poor and their spokesmen cannot in general be looked upon as allies of the new populism,"[18] i.e., the populism of such mass-based public interest groups as Common Cause and Public Citizen. He also points out that public interest groups have been attacked by Black leaders for focusing on issues that are of little concern to the poor.

True, the support for public interest groups has come predominantly from the upper middle class, but they never suggested that they oppose members (or contributors) from the lower middle class or from the poor. They have welcomed support from all Americans, but—as many studies have shown—members of the upper middle class are more likely to join an organization like Common Cause because they are more likely than are members of other classes to take an active interest in politics. We may want to question whether Common Cause indeed speaks for "the people," because most people have not chosen to join Common Cause, but we cannot accuse Common Cause—or Public Citizen for that matter—of having designed an agenda that advances only the interests of the upper middle class. If we look at some of the positions public interest groups have taken—from opposition to the war in Vietnam to opposition to nuclear power—it is not clear that they redound only to the benefit of upper middle-class, White professionals.

A more subtle criticism of public interest groups is that they have constituted a "new class" that wants more governmental intervention in the economy because then they will have more power and the business community will have less. The notion of class, however, is confusing because it implies that the ideas of those who support public interest groups arise out of—or are in some way related to—their interests, their economic well-being. But if power is what the "new class" is after, then it is not very helpful to call its constituents a class, for many people and groups have wanted power for reasons that have nothing to do with advancing their interests. Like the Federalists and the Mugwumps, the leaders of public interest groups have wanted to be powerful lobbyists because they are convinced that their prescriptions are necessary to heal a sick society.

Thus, it is misguided to attack public interest groups by saying that their disinterested stance is a a ruse, that behind their disinterested ideals lie less noble motives, lie calculations of self-interest. The most important characteristic of the leaders of public interest groups is their conviction that the wrong people—that is, self-interested people—are influential lobbyists in Washington. And the wrong people are influential mainly because of the money they wield, their contributions to the election campaigns of congressmen. "The most important goal," an official of Common Cause emphasizes, "is to end the influence of money on politics,"[19] especially the influence of corporate money. According to many spokesmen for public interest groups, corporate campaign contributions skew the legislative process, and corporations themselves are harming the nation and the people by producing dangerous products and damaging the environment. It is appropriate that the Commission for the Advancement of Public Interest Organizations, founded in 1974 "to investigate ways of enlarging the constituency and capabilities of the public interest movement,"[20] is supported by the Monsour Medical Foundation, which sponsors research in community and environmental health.

The idea that business in general—and in particular the large corporation—is making the United States sick is not a particularly radical one. It is in many ways a quintessentially American idea. As Irving Kristol points out: "No other institution in American history—not even slavery—has ever been so consistently unpopular as has the large corporation with the American public."[21] Many Americans, from farmers to small-town businessmen, have attacked big business; and well-educated professionals have been nourished on the writings of Twain, Henry Adams, and numerous journalists and novelists who have spoken of robber barons and corporate villains. Why, then, did the public interest groups suddenly flower at the end of the 1960s? The answer is Nixon and the war in Vietnam, which led even some corporate executives to question the health of the society. Many Americans responded to the call of Gardner and Nader not because their interests were at stake but because they thought that something must be done to heal the society. They were animated not by enlightened self-interest but by a profound disinterestedness, for the war in Vietnam and the crisis of Watergate were very disturbing to them—as indeed they were disturbing to most

Americans. But even if one has a different view of the motives of those who rallied to the public interest group movement, was the movement's diagnosis of the society's ills right?

In 1967, Mark Green, who subsequently became head of Nader's Congress Watch, did a daring thing while serving as a summer intern for Senator Jacob Javits: He circulated among his fellow interns a letter to President Johnson urging him to withdraw American troops from Southeast Asia. Johnson was enraged, and cancelled his customary meeting with summer interns. And Javits, who thought interns should not be drafting positions on foreign policy, contemplated dismissing Green. Like many well-educated young Americans, Green was profoundly opposed to the war and progressed from a strong antiwar stance to a strong antibusiness stance, for it was assumed that the "problem" of Vietnam was closely related to the problem of "monied special interests" in particular and the problem of corruption in general. Had not Maynard Mack, in his address to the Modern Language Association, suggested as much? If the issues were related, however, it was not clear to anyone exactly what the connection was. Both Gardner and Nader attacked the "money-heavy special interests," and both came out against the war in Vietnam, yet neither suggested that the war was actually caused by "money-heavy special interests" or was being prolonged by them.

Presumably, both Gardner and Nader knew that the most fervent supporters of the war had not been businessmen but policy intellectuals. In the early 1960s, such men as McGeorge Bundy, Dean Rusk, and Walt Whitman Rostow were convinced that if the United States "lost" Vietnam, it would lose all of Southeast Asia. China was the central problem, Rusk thought, and just before the Vietnam escalation in 1965, he stated that Peking's militant ideology reflected "appetites and ambitions that grow upon feeding."[22] In 1968, he equated the doctrine spewing out of Peking with *Mein Kampf.* Rusk was a former law professor and foundation executive. The policymakers most skeptical about pursuing a policy of escalation in Vietnam were Chester Bowles, a former advertising executive, and George Ball, a former stockbroker. And in 1968, the "Wise Men"—convened by President Johnson at Clark Clifford's behest—who opposed any further escalation were mostly bankers and lawyers. As Godfrey Hodgson puts it: "The establishment made a characteristic decision: not to send good money after bad."[23] In other words, the world of corporate power told the world of policymaking intellectuals—intellectuals from academe and the foundations—that the war had been a mistake.

We cannot say, then, that the war in Vietnam was in any way caused by corporate power, which Nader calls "the overriding issue of our times." Nor can we say that Rusk, Bundy, and Rostow recommended the escalation of the war because they were deliberately pursuing the policies of special interest groups. Their recommendations were surely motivated by a disinterested concern for the health of the country. The United States, they thought, would lose credibility as an ally if it did not stand up to the threat of Communist imperialism. Appeasement was an invitation to further aggression. If the United States did not contain communism in South Vietnam, then it would have to contain it somewhere else—perhaps at a greater cost. "The basic decision in Southeast Asia is here," Lyndon Johnson said in 1961, after a fact-finding tour, "We must decide whether to help these countries to the best of our ability or throw in the towel in the area and pull back our defenses to San Francisco."[24] His was not the voice of a fanatical hawk but the voice of most informed opinion at the time. President Kennedy spoke that same year of the "relentless pressures of the Chinese communists" in Southeast Asia. George Ball was one of the few advisers who disagreed. He said in 1964, "What we might gain by establishing the steadfastness of our commitments we could lose by an erosion of confidence in our judgment."[25] Neither Ball's nor Rusk's position, however, can be explained by pointing to either's close connections with corporate power. We can question the political and military judgment of those who advocated an escalation of the war in South Vietnam, but we cannot say that their "great decision" was made because of the undue influence of corporate power in particular or special interests in general. The positions people take on matters of foreign policy can rarely be explained by pointing to their interests.

For virtually all American policymakers, the central question of the post–World War II era was relations with the Soviet Union. Most policymakers supported containment in principle. Raymond Aron says of containment: "Insofar as the United States set itself a goal or sought a mission for itself after the Second World War, what other policy save containment was open to it after cooperation with Stalin had proved impossible? The Soviet Union, weakened though it had been by its sacrifices for the common cause, had replaced the Third Reich as 'the disturbing force,' a threat to the European equilibrium and, indeed, the world equilibrium."[26] But if most policymakers supported containment in principle, other equally disinterested policymakers disagreed about what containment should mean in practice. The war in Vietnam, which was the result of a particular interpretation of containment, may have made the society sick, but it made no sense to regard the war as something fostered by the power of special interests. Getting out of Vietnam, however, may have been the right course of action, even though it was based on a misdiagnosis of why we were there in the first place.

Aside from Vietnam, the public interest group movement has had little to say about foreign policy—or, for that matter, about defense policy. In a survey of periodicals put out by organizations it has designated as being in the public interest, the Commission for the Advancement of Public Interest Organizations lists only three newsletters that focus on foreign and defense policy, whereas it lists sixteen on environmental policy. The descriptions of the organizations that publish the former reveal that their agendas have been very similar: The Center for Defense Information "opposes excessive or wasteful expenditures or forces," and holds that "strong social, economic and political structures contribute equally to national security"; SANE supports the "conversion of military facilities, reduction of defense spending and reallocation of defense funds to domestic issues"; and the Coalition for a New Foreign and Military Policy hopes to "mobilize public support for a peaceful, noninterventionist, humanitarian and open U.S. foreign and military policy," and says that its major objective is "to cut wasteful and unnecessary defense and interventionist spending and transfer it to needed social and human welfare programs."[27] All three organizations have assumed that the sooner the United States reduces its expenditures for defense the better off all Americans will be.

Both Common Cause and Public Citizen have said little about defense and foreign policy. Common Cause lobbied against the war in Vietnam but it began quite early in its existence to focus on what it has called "structure and process" issues. In 1979, however, it made the ratification of SALT II one of its major lobbying concerns, and listed "defense spending" as one item on its lobbying agenda. Nader publicly opposed the war in Vietnam, but his organization has focused exclusively on domestic issues. A recent issue of *The Public Citizen,* its newsletter, makes no mention of foreign policy in its summary of the work Public Citizen did in the 1970s. The Citizens party, however, called for an "immediate, sharp reversal" in military spending.[28]

Why have public interest groups devoted so little time to defense policy and foreign policy? Perhaps the main reason is that they do not think either is as important as domestic policy. If we flesh out their position, it would closely follow the interpretation of American foreign policy offered by revisionist historians, who argue that "the dynamics of capitalism" have chiefly been responsible for the Cold War. Although Nader would not claim that big business dictates foreign policy, he would probably point to, as one revisionist historian puts it, "the close connections between the government's foreign policy elite and corporate business. . . ."[29] And he would also say, I suspect, that if the Citizens party, with its self-proclaimed "socialist-inspired" party platform, were to gain power, then the Cold War would wane, for the Soviet Union would then realize that the United States was no longer a nation controlled by large corporations. The USSR would therefore reduce its defense expenditures, which would ultimately enable the United States to sharply reduce its defense expenditures.

The notion that U.S. foreign policy can be explained in the main by invoking capitalism has been questioned by a number of historians. Hans Morgenthau asserts that "economic determinism as a guide to the understanding of American foreign policy was discredited long ago by case studies that showed the extent to which the so-called dollar diplomacy of the turn of the century . . . was a political policy using economic interests for the political purposes of the state rather than the other way around."[30] Moreover, during the past decade big business has not fostered the Cold War but promoted détente. Interested in the possibility of gaining new markets, large corporations have shown little reluctance to do business with Communist regimes. The strongest supporters of containment have been several labor unions, not large corporations. The above description of Nader's approach to foreign policy, however, is highly speculative because Nader has never spoken at length about the subject. Perhaps another reason for the public interest group movement's inattention to foreign and defense policy is its uncertainty that the positions taken on these questions by its adversaries can be explained by invoking the notion of corporate interest in particular or special interests in general.

Certainly the charge that business unduly influences domestic policy is more plausible than the charge that it influences foreign policy. On most questions of foreign policy, it is not clear where the interest of business lies, whereas on many questions of domestic policy business may have a clear sense of what policy (or policies) redound to its benefit. Clearly, business political action committees (PACs) contribute to the campaign of a candidate in the hope that if elected he or she will vote along lines they favor. "Contributions by PACs," an official of Common Cause maintains, "are contributions with a legislative purpose," and he cites a recent study to support his point that "PAC money is *interested* money."[31] To which one can only respond: Of course. Why else would corporations—or labor unions, educational associations, farm groups—contribute to a candidate's campaign?

The disclosure laws are such that the business community cannot deny it contributes to congressional campaigns, but it argues that the contributions as well as the money it spends for lobbying are signs of its weakness, not strength—signs of its relative lack of influence. Several independent observers agree with that assessment. A writer in the *National Journal,* for example, contends that the increase in business lobbying "stems directly from the increase in government laws and regulations that business groups, by and large, have opposed. . . ." The fact that the business community is more visible now than it was ten or fifteen years ago, he adds, "attests more to their weakness than anything else."[32] According to another observer, many businessmen regard themselves as relatively powerless in comparison with labor, agriculture, the academic community, and the press. Acknowledging that in the past ten years it has begun to increase significantly the amount it spends on lobbying—the Chamber of Commerce's annual lobbying budget is $30 million—the business community says that it has done so out of desperation, out of a sense that something must be done to change public opinion, which it regards as antibusiness.[33]

The question of influence is a tricky one. Some observers believe that in the mid-1970s the business community had very little influence but that by the close of the decade its influence had increased enormously, so that a writer in *The New York Times* could argue in December of 1979 that "the business community has quietly become the most influential lobby in Washington."[34] But the article cited in the previous paragraph appeared in the *National Journal* in February of 1980. Which journalist is right? In any case, the question of influence cannot be resolved merely by citing the business community's complaint that it has no influence. The business community must think that money does buy *some* influence; otherwise, why would it spend so much on campaign contributions? We should be skeptical of the claims of both the business community and the public interest groups, for it is in the interest of each to argue that the other is more influential—to argue, that is, that its point of view has not been sufficiently taken into account.

Public interest groups are especially dependent upon the notion of the undue influence of business because they will wither away unless they convince potential supporters that the sickness of the nation requires that more people take the high road of disinterest. (By contrast, lobbying groups for business—or any lobbying group that is concerned with looking out for its own interests—do not need to dwell so much on the dangers of other groups because it is rightly assumed that people will always support organizations that look out for their interests.) Yet, public interest groups are obliged to claim that they have been somewhat influential, lest potential supporters write them off as ineffectual. Thus public interest groups must maintain both that they are weak and that they have been strong. In a recent mailing campaign for members, Common Cause spoke of "urgently needed changes," and at the same time Archibald Cox said: "Even if you were not a member of Common Cause throughout its first ten years, you should be aware of the victories it achieved in your name and in the name of all its citizens."[35]

Even if we discount some of the boasts in the promotional literature of public interest groups, it is clear that they have been influential. Senator Edward Kennedy believes that Common Cause and Public Citizen have become "almost an extension of Congress," and former Senator Abraham Ribicoff points out that "instead of the big lobbyists of the major corporations dominating the hearings process, you have had practically every committee in Congress according equal time to public interest people."[36] Just how influential they were in the 1970s—and are now in the 1980s—will always be a matter of debate, but their astonishing success in the early 1970s undermines their contention that special interests distort the legislative process because of the money they wield. Mark Green claims that "eventually, not even the gale-force winds of corporate money and lobbyists can uproot the extremely broad, popular appeal . . . of the consumer-citizen community."[37] The movement has been successful because of its ability to mobilize public opinion in its favor, or at least in favor of its legislative agenda. As James Q. Wilson observes: "One cannot *assume* that the disproportionate possession of certain resources (money, organization, status) leads to the disproportionate exercise of political power."[38] The testimony of leading members of public interest groups as well as leading members of Congress makes it clear that public opinion—not money—is the most significant factor in politics.

But if Nader's and Gardner's diagnosis of domestic problems is not persuasive, it does not follow that their prescriptions are wrong. We do not have to subscribe to Nader's indictment of corporate power to acknowledge that product safety and the quality of the environment are legitimate subjects of political debate. Nader, however, has moved beyond these concerns. His prescription for domestic ills is not a battery of regulations but a change in the nature of the corporation. In 1980, Public Citizen published "The Case for a Corporate Democracy Act of 1980," a report that calls for "corporate governance reform." According to Public Citizen, "the proposal would make giant corporations more accountable to their various constituencies—consumers, workers, local communities, small businessmen—by democratizing the way these companies govern themselves."[39] Would such a radical change necessarily benefit the consumer? The reaction of one observer: "If a man described as a consumer advocate proposes to break up companies that have supplied products of proven excellence and acceptability, what would a 'consumer enemy' do?"[40] But the most obvious point is that the prescription does not follow from the diagnosis. The medicine, it seems, is much too strong for the disease, for a corporate democracy act would not simply reduce the influence of large corporations but eliminate it altogether.

If it is difficult to square Nader's prescription with his diagnosis, it is also difficult to see that Common Cause could agree with the idea of corporate democracy, for the result of Nader's proposal would be a vast expansion of the Special Interest State. The kind of stagnation that has become characteristic of the political world, where legislating has become difficult because it is hard to construct coalitions, would then become characteristic of the corporate world. But if two self-proclaimed public interest groups disagree —or at least appear to disagree; Common Cause has taken no position on corporate democracy—about what is in the public interest, then the notion that domestic problems could be resolved if everyone was disinterested is questionable. (The economists whose opinions are continually solicited on the matter of inflation often disagree about what should be done, not because they represent different interests but because they have different ideas about what is in the public interest.) The cultivation of disinterested-ness, then, is not the answer to domestic problems.

To some degree, disinterestedness may be part of the problem. As we have seen with the Federalists and the Mugwumps, men who stand upon their disinterest suffer from certain disabilities. Their disinterestedness tends to render them immune to the arguments of others as well as incapa-ble of modifying their views in light of new evidence. If Nader has the courage of his convictions, he also has the complacency of a man who is certain that his disinterestedness means that his policies are right. The leaders of the public interest movement pay no heed to Publius's warning in *Federalist* 1 that there is no relation between pure motives and prudent policy. Certain of their pure motives, the leaders of public interest groups are inclined to dismiss opposing points of view as those of venal or corrupt men—at the very least the views of politicians who act out of self-interest.

By questioning the motives of those who disagree with their prescrip-tions, the public interest groups foster a climate that is not conducive to deliberation. Even if a congressman has reason to think that a bill is foolish, he may be feel compelled to vote for it because he worries that voters will adjudge him corrupt if he does not do so. But when congressmen are more concerned with whether they look high-minded than with the merits of a particular piece of legislation, then deliberation suffers. Even Gardner him-self, after he left Common Cause, implied that public interest groups do not realize the importance of deliberation: "When equally unworthy groups want mutually incompatible things, unless you want to shoot it out or turn it over to a dictator, you've got to turn to the arena of politics. As you can imagine, *that is not the easiest idea to get across in good-government circles*" (emphasis added).[41] But it was Gardner himself, as well as Nader and other leading figures in the public interest group movement, who continually implied that most politicians are sadly lacking in concern for the public interest. As Gardner wrote: "There's a never-ending need for an organiza-tion that will keep the politicians honest"[42]—the implication being that were it not for Common Cause, most politicians would stray from the straight and narrow.

Convinced of their own purity of motive, the members of public interest groups tend to dismiss the arguments of those who disagree with them. This self-righteousness tends to make them doctrinaire, so that they persist in prescribing the same "reforms" of the political process. Their purity of motive, strangely enough, also makes them unpredictable, for the notion of acting in the public interest is a Pandora's box, out of which any stance on any issue can come. As a staff member of a Senate committee once said of Nader: "Nader is assuming the role of an Ajax white knight with no reins on the horse. My instinct is to distrust anyone who doesn't have to answer to a constituency."[43] Both Common Cause and Public Citizen, however, are predictable, insofar as they must remain wedded to their diagnoses in order to ensure the support of their members, but their prescriptions—that is, their legislative agenda—often have changed.

Some of Common Cause's difficulties are instructive. Several times its staff, which is responsible for "developing" issues, has recommended a policy on a substantive issue, only to find itself in trouble with either the governing board or the membership. The staff, for example, favored specific tax reform measures, and formulated a question on them for the annual referendum of members. The question was not approved by the governing board, which attacked it on several grounds. The result was the formation of a board committee to study what kind of tax reform measures Common Cause could support, but after one and a half years the committee was not able to come up with any recommendations. Disinterestedness did not lead to a clear prescription for tax reform.

On energy, Common Cause announced a policy, only to change its mind when a significant minority of the membership disapproved of it. According to an article in the Common Cause newsletter, Common Cause had developed "a balanced program for a national energy plan, with positions on nuclear power, coal, conservation, and imported oil. . . . But we came to realize that it just wasn't the right role for Common Cause." Not right because the organization had "veered too far afield from . . . traditional accountability issues. . . ."[44] But it was not the right role, it seems, because there was so much disagreement about what an appropriate energy policy should be. In 1978 Common Cause adopted the following energy policy: "Common Cause should work to remove institutional barriers to decision-making . . . ; Common Cause should work to ensure that decision-making is open, accountable and free from special interest pressures; Common Cause should work to ensure diversity and flexibility in our energy system by promoting conservation and alternative energy sources."[45] Only the third recommendation is substantive, but it is so vague that no member of Common Cause—indeed, no American—could possibly object to it.

Thus, Common Cause has found it difficult to move away from "structure and process" issues, for when it tries to take a substantive position it often generates too much dissension "in the ranks." To keep its members happy, then, it must continually stress that its central goal is reducing the influence of special interests. In a recent poll of its membership, Common Cause asked: "Do you favor or oppose Common Cause taking on the special interests directly by working in such areas as: A. Tax Reform, B. Military spending, C. Energy." Ninety-one percent of those who responded checked A, 75 percent checked B, and 88 percent checked C. What was being agreed on was *not* a particular policy with regard to tax reform, military spending, or energy but that Common Cause should "take on the special interests" in these areas. When Common Cause suggested specific policies with regard to energy, the membership was divided; and in the same referendum the membership virtually split on the question of whether there should be a moratorium on the construction of nuclear power plants.[46]

In the summer of 1979 Common Cause decided to support ratification of the SALT II treaty, although a significant number of members thought it an inappropriate issue for the organization. The treaty was not mentioned in the annual referendum, but a random poll of four thousand members revealed that only 66 percent favored lobbying for SALT II. Many members of the governing board also opposed the decision (the vote was 33 to 13). According to Fred Wertheimer, Common Cause had decided to support ratification because "the polls show that a majority of citizens support SALT, but the Senate is not getting that message. Instead, Senators are hearing from a vocal minority who oppose the treaty." Nan Waterman, head of the board, preferred to speak of the intrinsic merits of the issue: Common Cause has "an obligation to step outside its usual issues" due to the global significance of SALT. Finally, several board members invoked the notion of precedence; it was appropriate to support SALT II because Common Cause had once supported efforts to seek an end to the war in Vietnam.[47]

If Common Cause is essentially devoted, as both Gardner and Cohen have said, to "structure and process" issues, then its support for SALT II is puzzling. Yet, Gardner also stressed that Common Cause "has fought pitched battles on issues of the deepest concern to the American people— the Vietnam war, environmental pollution, racial injustice, poverty, unemployment, and women's rights."[48] And Common Cause has also lobbied against the supersonic transport plane (SST), the B-1 bomber, and bills weakening controls over air pollution and strip mining.[49] Common Cause, then, has been both rigid and unpredictable: rigid in its adherence to the notion that the undue influence of special interests has caused the sickness of the United States; unpredictable in that its positions on innumerable issues often bear little relation to its diagnoses.

Public Citizen's legislative agenda has been more predictable than Common Cause's, but its diagnosis of the sickness of the United States has never changed despite evidence that tends not to confirm it. The *Public Citizen,* for example, pointed out that as a result of the campaign finance reforms of 1974, a president was elected in 1976 who "is almost uniquely unbeholden to special interests." Yet, Nader, in explaining why he no longer supported President Carter even though Carter had appointed a number of Nader's associates to high positions, said that Carter had become "imprisoned by a matrix of corporate power." And Carter may well be viewed, Nader also said, "as the president who has done more damage to the consumer interest than any recent president."[50] How does a president unbeholden to special interests become a prisoner of corporate power?

If Common Cause and Public Citizen have exaggerated the influence of money on the political process, they have also exaggerated the "influence" of secrecy. Openness, Gardner holds, "ranks second to the rule of law as a necessary ingredient of self-government."[51] Both Common Cause and Public Citizen have played major roles in the passage of legislation to open up the government, and in transforming the operations of Congress. In 1972, for example, almost half of all House Committee meetings were closed to the public, whereas in 1975 only 3 percent were closed. Gardner takes credit for this: "We've opened up the bill-drafting sessions of the House of Representatives, which is just a profound change in their way of operating. You can walk in and out of that Ways and Means Committee while they're drafting your tax laws. And now that you can, it seems insane that they ever thought they could do the public business secretly."[52]

Although Gardner and Nader assume that a liberal democracy requires complete openness, the Founding Fathers—with the exception of Jefferson—thought otherwise. They were not, of course, in favor of closed government, but they thought there would be times when it might be prudent for a national legislature to deliberate in secret. Hamilton said of the Constitutional Convention that "had the deliberations been open while going on, the clamours of faction would have prevented any satisfactory result," and Madison believed that "the Constitution would never have been adopted by the Convention if the debates had been public."[53]

In an interview with Jared Sparks in 1830, Madison explained why he thought deliberation was best served by having a secret convention. It was best, he said,

> to sit with closed doors, because opinions were so various and at first so crude that it was necessary they should be long debated before any uniform system of opinion could be formed. Meantime the minds of the members were changing, and much was to be gained by a yielding and accommodating spirit. Had

the members committed themselves publicly at first, they would have afterwards supposed consistency required them to maintain their ground, whereas by secret discussion no man felt himself obliged to retain his opinions any longer than he was satisfied of their propriety and truth, and was open to the force of argument.[54]

Far from thinking that secrecy bred corruption, Madison thought that secrecy aided deliberation—that in complex matters of great moment, secrecy was useful because it enabled men to be open "to the force of argument."

Both Madison and Hamilton, then, did not think secret sessions of the national legislature antithetical to the spirit of republican government. Although the government, they might have said with Lincoln, is of the people, by the people, and for the people, it is a government in which the people do not directly participate. The people, according to the First Amendment, have the right "to petition the government for a redress of grievances," but they do not have the right to know about all the deliberations that take place in Congress. Although Article 1, Section 3, of the Constitution requires each House to keep a journal of its proceedings, it also allows that each House may leave out "such parts as may in their judgment require secrecy. . . ." The Founding Fathers did not extol secrecy, but neither did they rule it out. And they probably would have had grave reservations about the spate of laws enacted in the mid-1970s that make the American government the most open government in history.

Preoccupied with secrecy and corruption, with the supposed ability of monied special interests to buy the votes of congressmen—or at the very least to unduly influence the way they vote—the members of public interest groups have a cast of mind that is suspicious of politicians. They continually imply that politicians are a sleazy bunch who often betray the interests of the people. According to John Gardner, Common Cause is "a means of assuring continuous accountability to the citizen—a means of voting between elections. We think it's time to give this nation back to its people."[55] And Ralph Nader counsels that "with the increasingly apparent failure of our elected representatives to represent the people who pay all the bills in this country, we've got to regroup."[56] Both men claim that they want to restore trust in government, but the existence of their organizations depends upon their ability to convince Americans that they should always distrust those whom they choose to represent them—not simply to be skeptical of campaign rhetoric but generally to assume that positions taken are the result of self-interest, unless of course the positions are consonant with those of Common Cause or Public Citizen.

In many ways the rhetoric of the public interest movement, like the rhetoric of the Mugwumps, sounds like the patriotic rhetoric of men like Samuel Adams and Patrick Henry. Yet the latter-day men of little faith who support Public Citizen and Common Cause differ from their forebears in that they are ambivalent about making government as local as possible. As Washington-based organizations that consider lobbying on Capitol Hill one of their primary activities, both Common Cause and Public Citizen would be less influential if many issues were resolved not by Congress but by state or local governments. The gravest threat to their influence, it seems, is the movement for "direct democracy"—for such populist approaches to governance as referenda, initiatives, and recalls. Common Cause has not taken a position on the movement for direct democracy, yet Nader has come out in favor of it: "The legislative process is bankrupt; the initiative is the last bastion of democracy. . . ."[57] Direct democracy, however, may pose problems for the agenda of Common Cause and Public Citizen as well as undermine their influence, for most referenda and initiatives have come from the Right, whereas most supporters of public interest groups consider themselves on the Left.

Both Nader and Gardner reiterate how much they are for "the people," much more for "the people" than are the elected representatives. Yet, "the people" play virtually no part in selecting the agenda for political change of either organization. Common Cause does solicit its members' opinions before setting its lobbying agenda, but the organization itself sets out the choices in the questionnaire. In any case, usually only 10 percent to 15 percent of the membership responds. After the rankings are tabulated, the governing board, in consultation with the staff, decides to which issues Common Cause will devote most of its attention. Public Citizen's procedures have even less to do with "the people" than do Common Cause's. The organization has no members and no governing board; Nader and a number of key aides decide what its agenda will be. Both Common Cause and Public Citizen may speak for "the people," but they do so, as one observer puts it, "through the voices (and deliberations) of a very few."[58]

Public interest groups often imply that "the people" do not know what is good for them because they are manipulated by business advertising. In *Politic and Markets,* a book that has been praised by many public interest groups, Charles Lindblom argues that Americans have been indoctrinated by not only advertising but also the educational system. Elsewhere he claims that "the fabled 'competition of ideas' long held necessary to democracy is a grossly lopsided competition when the media are largely controlled by corporate business."[59] Certain that their own views are right—Lindblom continually says that his views coincide with those of "thoughtful people"—the supporters of public interest groups tend to dismiss the views of businessmen, congressmen, and "the people" themselves. "The people" have been deceived and indoctrinated; they have been taken advantage of by venal and unscrupulous forces, and are therefore benighted. The public interest groups are certain that they know what is best for "the people."

Common Cause, however, would deny that it is especially entitled to speak for "the people." "We are a citizens' lobby, a public interest group," an official of Common Cause emphasizes. "The difference between 'a' and 'the' is very important. We don't define 'the public interest' in the sense that one group represents it while others don't." And Gardner asserts that "no citizens' movement should assume that it has some divinely inspired grasp of what is 'in the public interest.' It must have the courage of its convictions, but it must present those convictions in the public forum where all other groups can debate their validity."[60] Yet, how can "all other groups debate their validity" when Common Cause impugns the motives of its opposition? Common Cause and Public Citizen may say that their ideas of what is in the public interest should be debated by all groups, but they clearly think that their ideas are entitled to much more respect and attention than the ideas, say, of a lobbyist for the oil industry.

Public interest groups regard themselves as essential to the political process, as indeed more representative than the "so-called"—to use Nader's term—representative institutions, but it is not quite clear what their role is in a representative democracy. Some observers suggest that the notion of civic balance best describes the function of public interest groups. That is, public interest groups act as a countervailing power to the special interests. But why should the views of organizations whose membership probably does not exceed a half-million persons be equally weighted with the views of lobbying groups whose memberships number in the millions—organizations such as farm associations, labor unions, educational associations, and business groups? Many Americans vaguely agree with Public Citizen that big business should be regarded with suspicion, and many Americans vaguely agree with Common Cause that legislators vote according to their contributions, but the public that actually supports the work of public interest groups is very small.

Other observers believe that public interest groups do not represent a vaguely defined public but "constituencies that have been chronically unrepresented or underrepresented in American politics."[61] But in what sense can we say that the upper-middle-class professionals who support public interest groups have been unrepresented or underrepresented in politics? It may be unfair to say that Common Cause and Public Citizen have an agenda that speaks to their interests, but it is not clear how the Common Cause or Public Citizen agenda reflects the interests of such underrepresented constituencies as Chicanos, Blacks, Native Americans, and Appalachian Whites.

Finally, some observers say only that public interest groups stand for "a significant point of view, which ought to be represented in the decision process, but which cannot command enough wealth or organizational resources to assure the necessary political response."[62] What is the point of view of public interest groups? No doubt, they agree with one another on most issues more than they agree with business lobbyists, but just as there is no uniform "business interest," there is no uniform public interest "point of view." A first-term congressman relates the following story: "I was walking from the elevator into the House to vote, and you know how the lobbyists line up along the hall there to tell you what they want. Well, about five of them were shouting at me to vote yes, and five more were shouting no. And all ten worked for public interest groups! I mean, so how am I supposed to know which vote is for the public interest?"[63] Those lobbying organizations that consider themselves public interest groups lack a significant point of view, if by significant we mean a point of view that is distinctively and uniformly their own.

The picture is further complicated by the rise of public interest groups whose agenda is often pro-business rather than pro-consumer—to use Congress Watch's terminology. The older public interest groups label these upstarts "so-called" public interest groups, but who is to say which public interest group is the "real" public interest group? The older public interest groups would advance themselves, of course, as the more legitimate pretenders to the title because they do not stand to benefit by their views. The distinction has very little meaning, for often what is good for a significant number of Americans—whether farmers, or workers, or businessmen—is thereby in the public interest. To some degree, as Publius says in *Federalist* 10, the public interest lies in formulating policies that benefit the numerous special interests that compose the country. Public interest groups are different from special interest groups because of the peculiar dynamics, as it were, of disinterest, but otherwise there is no real distinction between them. Public interest groups are special interest groups, and special interest groups are public interest groups. Each group, of course, has a right to lobby, but whether its proposals are in the public interest is a matter for Congress—and no other body—to determine.

Owing to their disinterestedness, which has made them rigid and unpredictable, will such public interest groups as Common Cause and Public Citizen suffer the fate of the Mugwumps, becoming anachronisms as public opinion, in effect, passes them by? It is too soon to tell, but it is clear that their influence is on the wane. In 1981, on the tenth anniversary of the creation of Public Citizen, the *Washington Post* reported that Nader's organization "has lost battles more frequently—even given up some ground—and its financial support has declined."[64] In 1980 Public Citizen raised only

$710 from direct mail solicitations. And in May, 1982 the *Post* ran a story on Nader in which the author said that "now some politicians say they like having it known that Nader doesn't like them. Many voters, they believe, don't like Nader." It was otherwise in the early 1970s: "Nader was often used by politicians in their campaign advertising"[65]—an association that at that time was considered a plus, a sign that the candidate was not beholden to special interests. According to several reports, Common Cause has suffered a similar loss of influence and dwindling of financial resources.

To compare the public interest groups of the 1970s to the Mugwumps, however, is misleading, because Common Cause and Public Citizen were highly successful lobbying organizations—organizations that in some ways profoundly affected politics in the 1970s—whereas the Mugwumps generally were ineffectual, having disdained lobbying. The Mugwumps considered themselves vindicated if public opinion was against them, whereas Public Citizen and Common Cause court public opinion. Both Common Cause and Public Citizen still have numerous supporters, and it is possible that their fortunes will improve if they seize upon issues that enable them to mobilize public opinion in their favor.

Notes

1. Cited, Paul Lutzker, "The Politics of Public Interest Groups: Common Cause in Action" (Ph.D. dissertation, Johns Hopkins University, 1973), p. 82.
2. Stephen Chapman, "In Common Cause," *Inquiry,* 5 March 1979, p. 9.
3. John Gardner, *In Common Cause* (New York: W. W. Norton, 1974), p. 41.
4. Cited, Robert F. Buckhorn, *Nader: The People's Lawyer* (Englewood Cliffs, N.J.: Prentice-Hall, 1972), p. 289.
5. Cited, John Gardner, *Morale* (New York: W. W. Norton, 1978), dustjacket.
6. Cited, Timothy B. Clark, "Public Interest Groups Show Their Age," *National Journal,* 12 July 1980, p. 1140.
7. See Godfrey Hodgson, *America in Our Time* (New York: Random House, 1978).
8. Andrew S. McFarland, *Public Interest Lobbies: Decision Making on Energy* (Washington, D.C.: American Enterprise Institute, 1976), p. 20.
9. Cited, Hodgson, *America in Our Time,* p. 364.
10. Maynard Mack, "To See It Feelingly," *ACLS Newsletter* 22 (1971):18–19.
11. Frances FitzGerald, *Fire in the Lake* (Boston: Little, Brown, 1972), p. 442.
12. Cited, T. R. Reid, "Public Trust, Private Money," *Washington Post Magazine,* 26 November 1978, p. 13.
13. Cited, Mack, "To See It Feelingly," p. 12.
14. See Chapman, "In Common Cause," p. 11.
15. Cited, ibid.
16. Ibid., p. 14.
17. Tom Bethell, "The 'Public Interest' Lobby," *Newsweek,* 24 April 1978, p. 23.
18. Simon Lazarus, *The Genteel Populists* (New York: Holt, Rinehart and Winston, 1974), p. 141.

19. Cited, Clark, "Public Interest Groups Show Their Age," p. 1141.
20. Brochure published by the commission.
21. Irving Kristol, "Corporate Capitalism in America," in *Two Cheers for Capitalism* (New York: Basic Books, 1978), p. 5.
22. Cited, Leslie H. Gelb and Richard K. Betts, *The Irony of Vietnam: The System Worked* (Washington, D. C.: Brookings Institution, 1979), p. 106.
23. Hodgson, *America in Our Time*, p. 359.
24. Cited, Arthur M. Schlesinger, Jr., *Robert Kennedy and His Times* (Boston: Houghton Mifflin, 1978), p. 725.
25. Kennedy and Ball cited, Gelb and Betts, *Irony of Vietnam*, pp. 71, 106.
26. Raymond Aron, *The Imperial Republic* (Englewood Cliffs, N.J.: Prentice-Hall, 1974), p. 300.
27. *Periodicals of Public Interest Organizations: A Citizen's Guide* (Washington, D.C.: Commission for the Advancement of Public Interest Organizations, 1979).
28. *New York Times,* 2 August 1979, sec. IV, p. 17.
29. Steven J. Cagney, letter to the editor, *New York Review of Books,* 20 March 1980, p. 44.
30. Cited, Arthur M. Schlesinger, Jr., reply to Cagney, ibid., p. 43.
31. Fred Wertheimer," in *Parties, Interest Groups, and Campaign Finance Laws,* ed. Michael J. Malbin (Washington, D.C.: American Enterprise Institute, 1980), p. 193.
32. Robert J. Samuelson, "What's Good for the Country," *National Journal,* 9 February 1980, p. 244.
33. See "Nader Study Claims Big Business Groups Manipulate Congress," *Washington Post,* 17 February 1980, p. A18.
34. Philip Shabecoff, "Big Business on the Offensive," *New York Times Magazine,* 9 December 1979, p. 134.
35. Common Cause brochure.
36. Cited, Timothy B. Clark, "The Public and the Private Sectors: The Old Distinctions Grow Fuzzy," *National Journal,* 1 January 1980, p. 101.
37. *Congress Watcher,* January/February 1980, p. 7.
38. *Wall Street Journal,* 11 January 1978, p. 14.
39. *Public Citizen: Annual Report, 1979* (unpaginated).
40. Robert Hessen, *In Defense of the Corporation* (Stanford: Hoover Institution Press, 1979), p. 97.
41. Cited, Tom Bethell, "Taking a Hard Look at Common Cause," *New York Times Magazine,* 24 August 1980, p. 44.
42. *Frontline* 4 (January-February 1978):2.
43. Cited, James Q. Wilson, *Political Organizations* (New York: Basic Books, 1974), p. 323.
44. Jan Leslie Cook, "Common Cause—How Do Your Issues Grow?" *Frontline* 4 (May-June 1978):6.
45. *Frontline* 5 (July-August 1979):1.
46. See *In Common* 10 (Spring 1979):28.
47. See *Frontline* 5 (July-August 1979):1, 3.
48. Gardner, *In Common Cause,* p. 18.
49. Anne White and Robert McIntyre, "Eight Years of Fighting for Tax Justice," *Public Citizen,* Winter 1980, p. 3.

50. Cited, *New York Times,* 12 August 1979, section IV, p. 2; *Washington Post,* 5 August 1979, p. F1.
51. Gardner, *Morale,* p. 97.
52. Interview with John Gardner, *Congressional Quarterly,* 15 May 1976, p. 1202.
53. Max Farrand, ed., *The Records of the Federal Convention of 1787,* 4 vols. (New Haven: Yale University, 1937), vol. 3, pp. 368, 479.
54. Ibid., p. 479.
55. Gardner, *In Common Cause,* p. 20.
56. *Washington Post,* 5 August 1979, p. F2.
57. Cited, H. Peter Metzger, *The Coercive Utopians: Their Hidden Agenda* (brochure published by the Public Service Company of Colorado), p. 9.
58. Jeffrey M. Berry, *Lobbying for the People: The Political Behavior of Public Interest Groups* (Princeton: Princeton University Press, 1977), p. 210.
59. Charles Lindblom, *Politics and Markets* (New York: Basic Books, 1978); *Capitalism, Socialism, and Democracy: A Symposium Reprinted from Commentary* (Washington, D.C.: American Enterprise Institute, 1978), p. 29.
60. "Public Interest Groups: Balancing the Scales," *Congressional Quarterly,* 15 May 1976, p. 1197.
61. Berry, *Lobbying for the People,* p. 288.
62. Lazarus, *Genteel Populists,* p. 154.
63. Cited, Reid, "Public Trust, Private Money," p. 18.
64. *Washington Post,* 13 September 1981, p. F1.
65. Juan Williams, "Return from Nadir," *Washington Post Magazine,* 23 May 1982, p. 14.

Conclusion: The Future of Special Interests

*For if you have embraced a creed which appears to be free from the
ordinary dirtiness of politics—a creed from which you yourself cannot expect to draw any material advantage—surely that proves that
you are in the right?*

—George Orwell

*It is the fashion among dilettantes and fops (perhaps I myself am
not guiltless) to decry the whole formulation of the active politics of
America, as beyond redemption, and to be carefully kept away from.
See you that you do not fall into this error.*

—Walt Whitman

Our survey of the politics of the 1790s, the Gilded Age, and the 1970s
leaves us with a general conclusion: On the national level, special interests
have been much less influential than their opponents have claimed. More
often than not political change in the United States has come about because
of changes in public opinion rather than pressure from special interest
groups. According to James Q. Wilson, "Fundamental political change has
not, since the Philadelphia convention of 1787, been the result of deliberation or moderation, but rather of the accumulation of elemental passions
that seek to redefine the principles of a good society and that arise out of
widely shared dissatisfactions rather than carefully tempered reflections."[1]
Wilson overstates his case when he speaks of "elemental passions," implying that Americans always have had a highly emotional approach to politics, but it certainly is true that we cannot make sense of American political
history by speaking only of how special interests have vied with each other
to influence the legislative process. Opinion, as Hume says, governs interest,
and we can never assume that by looking at someone's interests we can
know what his opinions will be. In 1773, Benjamin Franklin, who is often
regarded as a complacent defender of self-interest, denounced Parliament
for believing that only "interest" motivated people and that reducing the

price of tea 3d. per pound "is sufficient to overcome all the patriotism of an American."[2]

What should we make, then, of those who clamor for political reform in order to curb the power of special interests? It would be wrong to question their genuine concern for the health of the polity, wrong to accuse them of hypocrisy, but we have seen that they have exaggerated the influence of special interests—exaggerated especially the effect money has on the political process. As Norman Ornstein says: Congress has often been criticized "for being *too* responsive . . . to single, narrow interests. But more frequently, Congress' actions or inactions represent the consensus—or lack thereof—in the country at large. . . . Where and when there has been a national consensus, Congress has acted reasonably quickly and reasonably well. . . ."[3] Moreover, we have seen that those reformers who wrap themselves in the mantle of disinterest often make the difficult art of legislating even more difficult because they poison the air with speculations about the motives of their adversaries. And their tendency to dismiss the arguments of those who disagree with them because the arguments supposedly are based upon private interest usually makes them intellectually complacent and rigid—immune to new ideas or to modifying their own ideas. In short, as Henry Fairlie remarks, "Politics is far too serious to be left to the disinterested."[4]

Should nothing, then, be done to curb the power of special interests? Many observers take this position. They say that by giving money to PACs, special interests are exercising their First Amendment right "to petition the government for redress of grievances." Special interests are legitimate, they argue, and there is nothing sinister about their spending money to influence the course of government. In any case, special interests do not control Congress. As a Democratic congressman from northern Virginia reported to his constituents: "Personally I have not found the much touted special interests particularly difficult to deal with. Good lobbyists can be a quick source of accurate and relevant information and do provide a useful means by which large groups of citizens can petition their government for action. As long as all lobbyists are clearly identified and one knows who pays them, and there are penalties against deliberate misinformation and improper practices, the mischief they can do is minimal."[5]

It is tempting to call the problem of special interests a nonproblem, but I do not think we can, for even if special interests are less influential than some observers allege, many Americans think they are influential; many Americans think that Congress is filled with people who are beholden to special interest groups. What we have to worry about is not so much the real power of special interests but their presumed power, worry about it because the result of such perceptions may be an increase in political jealousy—that is, the suspicion that those holding public office are not serving the public interest but only their own private interest in either gaining wealth or remaining in power or both. As Rep. Philip Sharp of Indiana recently put it, "I'm not really worried about my own personal integrity in making an independent judgment, but I am concerned about the question of the perception of me and of the institution." Speaking to the New York State ratifying convention in 1788, Alexander Hamilton praised the spirit of jealousy as appropriate during the revolutionary war; it was what Americans needed to motivate them to fight against the supposedly corrupt British government. But he warned that jealousy was not appropriate to the postwar era because it might prevent the government from acquiring "strength and stability . . . and *vigor* in its operations."[6] It may be that unless Congress makes some attempt to deal with the supposed influence of special interests, political jealousy in the United States will increase to such a degree that there will be more and more calls for populist measures of decision making that will weaken the ability of Congress to carry out its intended functions.

Political jealousy has always been a problem in American politics. Those who opposed the Constitution thought an extended commercial republic unworkable in part because they thought it was bound to increase political jealousy. In a large republic, an Anti-Federalist writer said, the people "will have no confidence in their legislature, suspect them of ambitious views, be jealous of every measure they adopt, and will not support the laws they pass." The Federalists, on the other hand, thought political jealousy could as easily destroy even state governments, since jealousy made all but the most local of governments unworkable. In *Federalist* 55, Madison attacked "indiscriminate and unbounded jealousy" as a force that was ultimately destructive of representative government.

Even though the Federalists won the day, political jealousy has remained a strong strain in American politics. Yet, jealousy did not undermine the Framers' scheme of government because until recently the national government did not loom large in most people's lives. Pursuing their self-interest, many Americans were indifferent to the doings of government. During the past fifty years, however, the scope of the national government has grown a great deal. (In the past ten years public spending outpaced inflation by some 30 percent.) As a result, a vastly increased number of Americans are very much interested in what government does, interested because their interests are directly affected by government programs. This heightened interest in government affairs puts a great burden on Congress, in that many Americans invariably regard any change in any program as a sign of heartlessness or, more commonly, venality. Far from creating trust in government, the expansion of the scope of government has bred distrust and resentment. There is suspicion that some special interests are more influential than others, or that special interests in general shape the course of legislation. No doubt, many Americans agree with Mark Green and Jack Newfield who wrote in "Who Owns Congress?" that "one way or another, special interests have managed to dominate Congress because Congress decides who gets subsidies, who gets price supports, who gets regulated, who gets funded, who gets taxed, who gets tax exemptions, deferrals, credits and deductions—in short, who gets rich."[7]

Jealousy increases not only when the scope of government expands but also when the amount of money spent on campaigning for office continues to increase. In August 1982, the *Washington Post* reported that "the more than 3,000 political action committees have raised more than $138 million and spent about $105 million since January, 1981."[8] In 1964 campaign spending for all races totaled about $200 million; in 1980 it jumped to $900 million. The public generally assumes that to raise enough money to run for office, candidates—unless they are personally wealthy—must make promises to special interests. Not a week goes by without word from the press and public interest groups about the close correlation between a congressman's voting record and the legislation favored by the PACs from which he had received a good deal of money in campaign contributions. For example, an op-ed piece in the *New York Times* in August 1982 pointed out that the congressman who sponsored a bill favored by the National Beer Wholesalers Association had received a $5,000 campaign contribution from the association's political action committee, a trip to Las Vegas for himself and his wife, and a $1,000 honorarium for a speech.[9] Journalists quickly ferret out such connections on the most arcane pieces of legislation, and uncover questionable uses of funds supposedly intended for campaign expenses. In August 1982, the *New Republic* ran a cover story that claimed dozens of congressmen used campaign contributions for purposes that had little, if anything, to do with reelection campaigns.[10] A shadow, it seems, hangs over Congress—the shadow of too much money floating around; it is not only being used for questionable purposes but also compromising the integrity of the legislative process.

It is not easy to know what can be done to dispel that shadow. Although polls continually reveal that Americans have little confidence in Congress as an institution, there has been little support for the public financing of congressional campaigns. Even if such a law is passed, it probably would not limit the influence of special interests, especially because the Supreme Court has ruled that independent expenditures by committees or individuals are legal as long as they are made with no coordination with the candidate's campaign. A truly rigorous campaign finance law would probably be regarded by the Supreme Court as unconstitutional, for it would be con-

23

strued as limiting the free speech of candidates or of persons who want to make known to the general public their views about candidates. Moreover, such a law would probably favor incumbents because challengers usually need to spend more money than incumbents to advance their candidacies. Almost no one is happy with current campaign finance laws, but aside from Common Cause and Public Citizen few have an interest in changing them. As a reporter in the *Washington Post* said in July 1982: "These days there is about as much enthusiasm for campaign spending reform as for national health insurance, which is to say none at all. It is a cause without a constituency. Also, alas, it is a problem without an obvious solution."[11]

Some observers believe that politicians would be less vulnerable to the blandishments of special interests if political parties were stronger. The parties, they argue, reward special interest groups for disciplining themselves, for accepting that they have to find some common ground with other special interest groups within the fold of the party if their calls are to be heeded. Strong political parties protect congressmen by making them less dependent upon special interest groups for campaign funds and—more important—votes. But for many people, parties are part of the problem, not part of the solution; they are regarded as the breeding ground of professional politicians, people who make deals rather than exercise independent judgment. Since the 1930s party affiliation has declined while the number of persons who declare themselves independents has gone up—from 17 percent in 1937 to 32 percent in 1979.

Some observers see the 1980 election as the beginning of a resurgence of the political party, but others think that the number of independents is likely to continue to increase. Television, computerized mailing lists, and higher levels of education are often given as reasons for the decline in party affiliation. Even if the number of independents does not grow, more and more candidates are probably going to run quasi-independent election campaigns. Supported by a small army of enthusiasts, a candidate may assume that he has a better chance of winning a primary if he attacks party regulars for "selling out," for seeking compromises on issues.

But it would be wrong to blame the reforms of the 1970s for transforming the congressman into an isolated political entrepreneur who is responsive to his constituents as well as to special interests. The extraordinary expansion of congressional staffs in recent years has made it more difficult for Congress to engage in deliberation about issues. And new technologies have made it more difficult for congressmen to insulate themselves from special interest groups, who avail themselves of computer-based mass-mailing techniques to generate support for their concerns and to watch how congressmen vote. Even the ease of air travel puts pressure on congressmen to return often to their districts, where they serve as ombudsmen rather than national legislators. If Congress is a place of "buzzing confusion,"[12] so too may be the mind of the congressman; he is harassed by constituents, hounded by lobbyists, and bewildered by the excessive information furnished him by a bloated and energetic staff. In such a state, he is vulnerable to special interests, not necessarily because of their campaign contributions but because they are adept at explaining why their position is the right one to take. He is too worn out and burdened with other matters to devote much thought to the issue.

Perhaps too much attention has been paid to the problem of special interests and not enough to the problem of being a national legislator. Of course, the two cannot be separated, but shouldn't we worry less about making special interests weaker and more about making legislators stronger? For several reasons, the plight of the congressman has been neglected. Reformers have tended to look down on the politician as someone who makes deals, who lacks principles. ("To my mind," Ralph Nader says, "politics is too full of compromises that should not be made.")[13] On the other hand, political scientists have tended to focus instead on the dynamics of interest group pluralism. According to David Truman, theorists of interest group pluralism think that "governmental actors . . . are no more than referees of group conflict, registers of group demands, or ratifiers of the outcome of intergroup contests. The initiative for action (or inaction) is regarded as being exclusively with the groups; and governmental actors are assigned an almost wholly passive role."[14] By making a diminished thing of the political vocation, the theorists have given spokesmen for public interest groups the opportunity, as it were, to claim that Congress responds only to the concerns of special interests whereas public interest groups respond to the concerns of the people. More important, the limited notion of the legislator's function offered by many political scientists may reinforce the low esteem many Americans accord the professional politician.

The political vocation has never been highly regarded by Americans. In his *Autobiography,* Anthony Trollope writes of how his American friends "speak of public life as a thing apart from their own existence, as a state of dirt in which it would be an insult to suppose that they are concerned.' "[15] Politicians are regarded as either sneaky fellows who sell out to special interests or people who do nothing but have a good time in Washington. And the relatively low status of politicians probably has made many ambitious and talented people think twice before running for office. It may be that public financing of congressional campaigns will make it easier to attract candidates, as Publius put it, "whose wisdom may best discern the true interest of their country." But my concern is less with specific measures than with the cumulative effect of all the reform measures intended to ensure that congressmen remain honest. In August 1982, James

A. Miller, a special assistant to Senator Howard Baker, Jr., wrote that "recently, serving in Congress has turned into such an aggravating, exhausting and generally exasperating hassle, it's a wonder anybody wants to do it. Perhaps never before in political history have so many sacrificed so much for so little that was supposed to be so much." Being a congressman "has become nothing less than an endurance test," and thus there is "a perceived decline in the number of qualified and committed people. . . ."[16] Many congressmen would agree with Miller. They believe that for a variety of reasons serving in Congress has become so vexatious that "it's becoming very difficult to get good, substantial, successful people to enter public life."[17] And they argue that the post-Watergate "reforms" have "changed not only the way that Congress does business but the very type of individual likely to be elected to Congress," depriving government "of the sprinkling of 'agreeable villains' it needs."[18] Surely, to increase the probability that talented people will run for the office, we should err on the side of trusting congressmen too much rather than too little. As it stands now, they are expected to be—as Common Cause would put it—"continuously accountable," expected also to be "the complaint window in the Federal department store,"[19] expected finally to be angelic in their financial dealings.

The authors of *The Federalist* understood the danger of unremitting suspicion of legislators. Indeed, the main point of *The Federalist* is not that the flowering of special interests would make it unlikely that any one interest—or majority faction—would dominate the Congress and subvert the liberty of other Americans. The main point of *The Federalist* is the need for Americans to trust those whom they choose to represent them. Herbert Storing stresses: "All the Federalists insisted that there must be some degree of confidence in rulers. . . . The Federalist position was that jealousy of rulers must be kept within some kind of bounds. . . ." Or, as one Federalist writer cautioned: "Mean jealousy and groundless distrusts . . . in some measure authorize [our representatives] to betray their trust."[20] The prevalence of political jealousy, we might also say, encourages candidates for office to stir up that base emotion, in essence, to run against those in Washington. Finally, the prevalence of political jealousy encourages those in office, Richard Fenno holds, to "build constituent trust" by inviting constituents to blend their cynicism about Congress with his.[21]

The Federalists also argued, as we have seen, that national legislators would be more likely to be men of talent and civic virtue than would state legislators. National legislators rarely have been the paragons that Publius hoped they would be, but have they not been more able practitioners of legislating than their peers in the statehouses? Most historians would say that they have, and would also say that special interests have been much more influential at the state and local level than in Washington. We should be wary, then, of calls for a devolution of power, for more decision making by state and local governments. Although in some cases such devolution is reasonable, it would be foolish to assume that state and local officials should enjoy our confidence more than do national legislators. It makes little sense to assume that a state is, so to speak, a small republic whose people are homogeneous, so that civic virtue can flourish better there than in Washington.

To some degree we should repose more trust in national legislators than in state legislators because they are generally more ambitious, more desirous of fame and power. Like the Anti-Federalists, most Americans look askance at ambitious men, supposing that they are always out to arrogate power to themselves by any means. The Federalists thought otherwise. Ambitious people could be dangerous to the nation, but ambitious people could also be great political leaders. They would have agreed with Tocqueville: "It thus happens that ambition makes a man care for his fellows, and in a sense, he often finds his self-interest in forgetting about himself. I know that one can point to all the intrigues caused by an election, the dishonorable means often used by candidates, and the calumnies spread by their enemies. . . . These are great ills, no doubt, but passing ones, whereas the benefits that attend them remain."22 Have not all great American politicians— Madison, Hamilton, Jefferson, Lincoln, Roosevelt, and no doubt many others—been men of strong ambition?

What, then, is to be done? In an interview in the fall of 1982, Rep. Richard Bolling, the chairman of the House Rules Committee who was retiring after thirty-four years in Congress, spoke of the need for "major reform." He called for partial public financing of congressional campaigns in order to reduce the impact of money on politics: "Money and politics can destroy democracy in the United States." But he also spoke of the need to do something about "the perverse line of reform that resulted in the enormous increase in the subcommittees."23 Whatever reforms or—to use a more neutral word—changes Congress contemplates, it should keep in mind that their main purpose is not to placate those who suffer from political jealousy but to make deliberating less difficult and legislating less burdensome. The way to curb the power of special interests—a power that has been exaggerated—is not to try to eliminate their influence altogether. "Politics can be improved," Herbert Alexander allows, "but it probably cannot be sterilized and purified to a degree that reformers seek."24 The way to curb the power of special interests is to make the daily life of the congressman less of an ordeal than it is now, so that a career in politics will attract people of talent and ambition—people whose love of fame will give them the courage to say to their constituents, as Burke said to his, "Your representative owes you, not his industry only, but his judgment; and he betrays, instead of serving you, if he sacrifices it to your opinion."[25] Only a strong Congress, composed of talented and ambitious people, will be able effectively to *regulate,* to use Publius's word, special interests.

Notes

1. "Reagan and the Republican Revival," *Commentary,* October 1980, p. 27.
2. See Bernard Bailyn, *The Ordeal of Thomas Hutchinson* (Cambridge: Harvard University Press, 1974), pp. 379–80.
3. Norman J. Ornstein, "The House and the Senate in a New Congress," in *The New Congress,* ed. Thomas E. Mann and Norman J. Ornstein (Washington, D.C.: American Enterprise Institute, 1981), p. 382.
4. *Washington Post,* 21 September 1980, p. D4.
5. Joseph L. Fisher (Tenth District, Va.), "Report from Congress," June 1980, p. 4.
6. Sharp cited in Elizabeth Drew, "Politics and Money," *New Yorker,* 6 December 1982, p. 128; Hamilton cited in Herbert Storing, *What the Anti-Federalists Were For* (Chicago: University of Chicago Press, 1981), p. 71.
7. *Washington Post Magazine,* 8 December 1980, p. 10.
8. See David Burnham, "Inactive Reactors: One Year's Toll of Three Mile Island," *New York Times,* 16 March 1980, p. 1F.
9. Jay Angoff, "For Beer Drinkers," *New York Times,* 15 August 1982, p. 27.
10. Bill Hogan, Diane Kiesel, and Alan Green, "The New Slush Fund Scandal," *New Republic,* 30 August 1982, pp. 21–25.
11. Walter Shapiro, "And the Rich Shall Inherit Congress," *Washington Post,* 11 July 1982, p. C2.
12. On the growth of congressional staffs, see Michael J. Malbin, *Our Unelected Representatives* (New York: Basic Books, 1980); Roger H. Davidson, "Subcommittee Government: New Channels for Policy Making," in Masen and Ornstein, *The New Congress,* p. 131.
13. Cited, Buckhorn, *Nader,* p. 271.
14. David Truman, "Introduction to the Second Edition," in *The Governmental Process: Political Interests and Public Opinion* (New York: Alfred A. Knopf, 1981), p. xxv.
15. Anthony Trollope, *An Autobiography* (Garden City: Doubleday, n.d.), p. 237.
16. "The Capitol Hill Hassle," *Newsweek,* 23 August 1982, p. 9.
17. Former Rep. Otis G. Pike, *New York Times,* 27 March 1978, p. A15.
18. Former Rep. Michael Harrington, in *Wall Street Journal,* 21 September 1978, p. 31.
19. *New York Times,* 27 March 1978, p. A15.
20. Storing, *What the Anti-Federalists Were For,* p. 51; ibid.
21. Cited, "Watching Incumbents: One Study," *Congressional Quarterly,* 7 July 1979, p. 1354.
22. Alexis de Tocqueville, *Democracy in America,* ed. J. P. Mayer (Garden City: Doubleday, 1969), vol. 2, p. 510.
23. *Washington Post,* 26 September 1982, p. B3.
24. Herbert Alexander, "Political Finance Regulation in International Perspective," in *Parties, Interest Groups, and Campaign Finance Laws,* ed. Michael J. Malbin (Washington, D.C.: American Enterprise Institute, 1980), p. 352.
25. *Edmund Burke on Government, Politics, and Society,* ed. B. W. Hill (New York: International Publications Service, 1970), p. 157.

Index

Communism, 92, 102, 120
Competition, 91, 94
Congress, United States: civil service re-
form and, 97, 98, 101; corruption and,
1–2, 51, 87–88, 90, 129; immigration/
labor policies and, 104; in the Gilded
Age, 88–89; in the 1970s, 141–45; pub-
lic confidence in, 2, 139, 40. *See also*
Campaign finance; Party system
Conkling, Roscoe, 86, 98, 101
Constitution, United States, 33–34, 37, 72,
139; Beard's comments on the, 47–48;
Federalists' attitude toward the, 77–78;
Madison's attitude about the, 35; ratifi-
cation of the, 29, 34, 35, 38, 41–42, 51–
52, 54–55. *See also Federalist, The*
Corporations. *See* Business/Commerce
Corruption: Adams (Henry) on, 86, 87;
Congressional, 1–2, 51, 87–88, 90, 129;
Gilded Age and, 85, 87, 107; Henry
(Patrick) on, 65; in France, 74; in 18th
century America, 25, 30, 38, 49, 51, 82;
in 18th century Britain, 11–12, 26; in
the 1970s, 115, 116; Machiavelli on, 56;
Social Darwinism and, 94. *See also* Civil
service reform
Cox, Archibald, 116, 123
Croker, Richard, 96
Curtis, George W., 85

Dante, Alighieri, 55
Dart, Justin, 3–4
Darwin, Charles, 93
Deference, notion of, 26
Democracy, 5, 107, 130
Democrat Societies, 80
Democratic Party, 90, 100. *See also* Party
system
Descartes, René, 13, 21
Disclosure laws, 122
Disinterest, politics of, ch. 5 (85–111); civil
service reform and the, 96–101; criti-
cism of the, 95–96, 125–26; election of
1884 and the, 100; fatalism of the, 94;
immigration/labor policies and the, 102
–104, 105, 106; professional politicians
and the, 85–86, 90–91, 100, 101; role of
the, 104–105, 107, 132, 138. *See also*
Laissez faire
Donovan, Hedley, 115

Drew, Elizabeth, 3
Dreyfus, Jack, 117

Ely, Richard, 95
Emerson, Ralph Waldo, 81
Energy policy, 126
Evolution, 94

Fairlie, Henry, 138
Federalism: Hamilton and, 29, 30–32, 43,
76, 77, 78; Madison and, 29–32, 43, 51.
See also Federalist, The; Federalist
Party
Federalist Party, 66, 69, 72, 74, 75, 77, 79–
81, 109, 118, 139; attitude about the
Constitution of the, 77–78. *See also*
Hamilton, Alexander
Federalist, The, 7–8, 23, 34–43, ch. 3 (47–
60), 66–67, 79–80, 81–82, 109, 142, 143;
authors of, 7, 34, 42, 54, 68; Paper 1,
36, 38, 40, 125; Paper 10, 31, 32,
40, 47, 48, 49, 52, 56–57, 68, 132;
Paper 11, 66; Paper 14, 37; Paper 24, 66;
Paper 37, 33–34, 37; Paper 41, 67;
Paper 49, 36; Paper 51, 33, 48, 49, 50,
52, 68; Paper 55, 49, 50, 139; Paper 56,
51; Paper 57, 50, 52, 55; Paper 62, 36,
37; Paper 63, 53, 54; Paper 71, 54; Paper
85, 37–38, 39; views about foreign policy in, 66, 67; views about patriotism,
33–34, 36, 37–41, 57; views about
republicanism in, 31, 32, 37, 39–40, 49–
50; views about special interests, 7–8,
40–41, 48, 56–58; views about the political process in, 86
Fenno, Richard, 143
First Amendment, 129, 138
FitzGerald, Frances, 115
Foreign policy, American, 66–67, 121–22.
See also SALT II; Soviet Union; Vietnam
Fortune, 115
France: corruption in, 74; United States attitude toward, 64, 67–68, 70–74, 76, 79,
80. *See also* French Revolution
Franklin, Benjamin, 137–38
French Revolution, 63, 66, 67, 71, 74, 79,
81. *See also* France

Republicanism: definition of, 31; in *The Federalist*, 31, 32, 37, 39–40, 49–50; Jefferson's views about, 77; Madison's attitude toward, 31–32, 54, 68–69, 77
Rhetoric, 35–37, 38, 41, 129–30
Ribicoff, Abraham, 124
Robison, John, 78–79
Rohan, Duc de, 13, 21
Roosevelt, Theodore, 100
Rostow, Walt, 119
Rothman, David, 87, 106
Rousseau, Jean Jacques, xi, xii
Rusk, Dean, 119, 120
Rutland, Robert A., 41

SALT II, 121, 127
SANE, 121
Schurz, Carl, 97
Secrecy, 128–29
Sharp, Philip, 139
Sherman Antitrust Act (1890), 102
Skinner, Quentin, 56
Smith, Adam, 20, 21, 23, 30, 93
Social Darwinism, 93–94
Soviet Union, 120, 121–22
Sparks, Jared, 128
Special interests. *See* Interests, special
Spencer, Herbert, 93. *See also* Social Darwinish
Spoils system, 96, 98, 99, 101. *See also* Civil service reform
States' rights: Madison's views about, 77; Patrick Henry's views about, 28–29, 41, 42, 51, 64–65
Storing, Herbert, 29, 30, 43, 143
Sumner, William Graham, 94–95
Synar, Michael L., 4, 5

Tariff Act (1792), 65
Tariff policy, 89, 92
Tax reform, 126
Tilden, Samuel J., 97, 106
Tocqueville, Alexis de, 43, 144
Trimmer, 15–16
Trollope, Anthony, 142
Truman, David, 48, 142
Twain, Mark, 2

Unions. *See* Labor relations in the Gilded Age

Vietnam, 114, 115, 118, 119–20
Virginia Plan, 32
Virginia Resolution, 76, 77, 80

Wall Street Journal, 4, 114
Walpole, Robert, 11, 12, 28
Washington Post, 3, 4, 132, 133, 140, 141
Washington, George, 30, 35, 42, 71, 80
"Watchman, The," 25, 38
Watergate, 115, 118
Waterman, Nan, 127
Webster, Noah, 70, 75, 78
Wertheimer, Fred, 3, 6, 127
Wilkes, John, 11, 17, 23, 26–27
Will, George F., 56
Wilson, James Q., 124, 137
Wilson, Woodrow, 88
Wirth, Timothy E., 4, 36, 51

XYZ affair, 74